Suinescamp To Swanscombe

Then and Now

And the people who lived there

Including

Past & Present Photographs

Written Edited & Produced by

Mason Durling
&
Christoph Bull

An environmentally friendly book printed and bound in England by www.printondemand-worldwide.com

This book is made entirely of chain-of-custody materials

www.fast-print.net/store.php

SUINESCAMP TO SWANSCOMBE
Copyright © Mason Durling & Christoph Bull 2014

ISBN: 978-178456-052-2

All rights reserved

No part of this book may be reproduced in any form by photocopying
or any electronic or mechanical means, including information storage
or retrieval systems, without permission in writing from both the
copyright owner and the publisher of the book.

The right of Mason Durling & Christoph Bull to be identified as the author of this work has
been asserted by them in accordance with the Copyright, Designs and
Patents Act 1988 and any subsequent amendments thereto.

A catalogue record for this book is available from the British Library

First published 2014 by
FASTPRINT PUBLISHING
Peterborough, England.

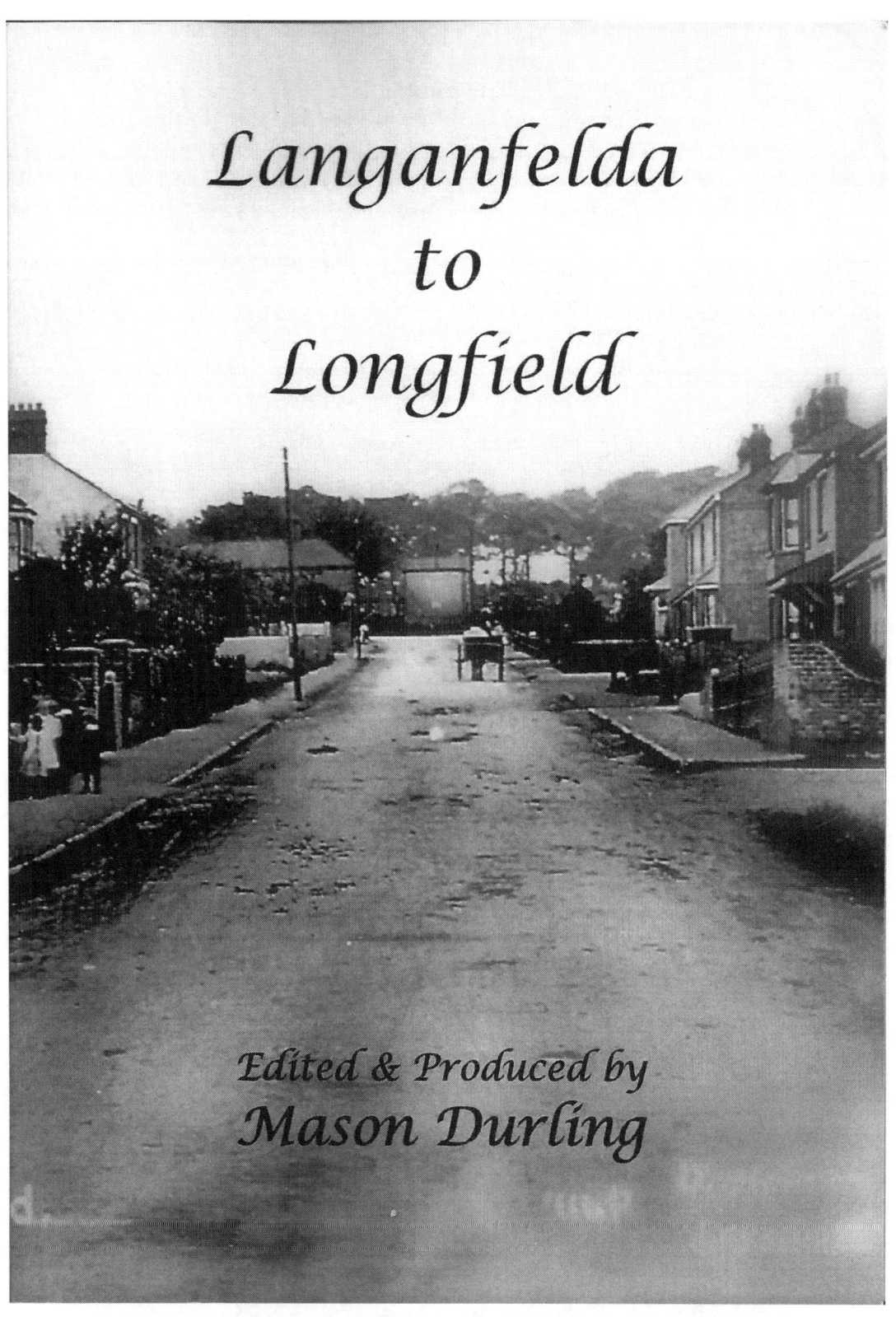

Available to buy or to download to your Kindle from Amazon

Dedicated to and in Memory of

Alfred William Durling 1852-1920
Ellen Ann (Mead) Durling 1848-1924
George Edward Durling 1879-1935
Florence Maud (Edgley) Durling 1881-1962
Frederick Charles Durling 1902-1975
Sarah Lilian (Beacon) Durling 1901-1983
George James William Durling BEM 1900-1980
Richard Michael Durling 1928-1978
George James Durling 1933-1939
(Peg) Kathleen (Fuertig)(Smith) Durling 1931-1991
Lived & Died in Swanscombe

Acknowledgements

I would like to thank the following for their assistance in making this book possible.

Christoph Bull for helping me put this book together, the use of his wealth of information on Swanscombe and without whom would have made my task on this project very difficult.
Gary Vaughan: For the use of his collection of Photographs and Postcards
Swanscombe fire service, for their cooperation with the fire service chapter.
I have tried to where I can to acknowledge people who have contributed material in this book either with their knowledge or without. Some of the information I have discovered is very old so it is very difficult to find these people or even if they are still around, I am sure that if any relatives of people who see a face or a name they know will be pleasantly surprised they have been immortalized in print. I discovered this when I published my Longfield book people telling me this was my uncle or aunt or grandparents and so on, and how lovely is was to see them mentioned. So if you do see anyone you know I hope you feel the same.
Peter Gear for the use of his memory and information on the shops and wartime memories
To my Dad for showing me where things were and telling me his stories and for always being there.
Also to my Aunt Jean who also gave me information about her school life and growing up in Swanscombe.
For my Family
X-X-X

Swanscombe 1897

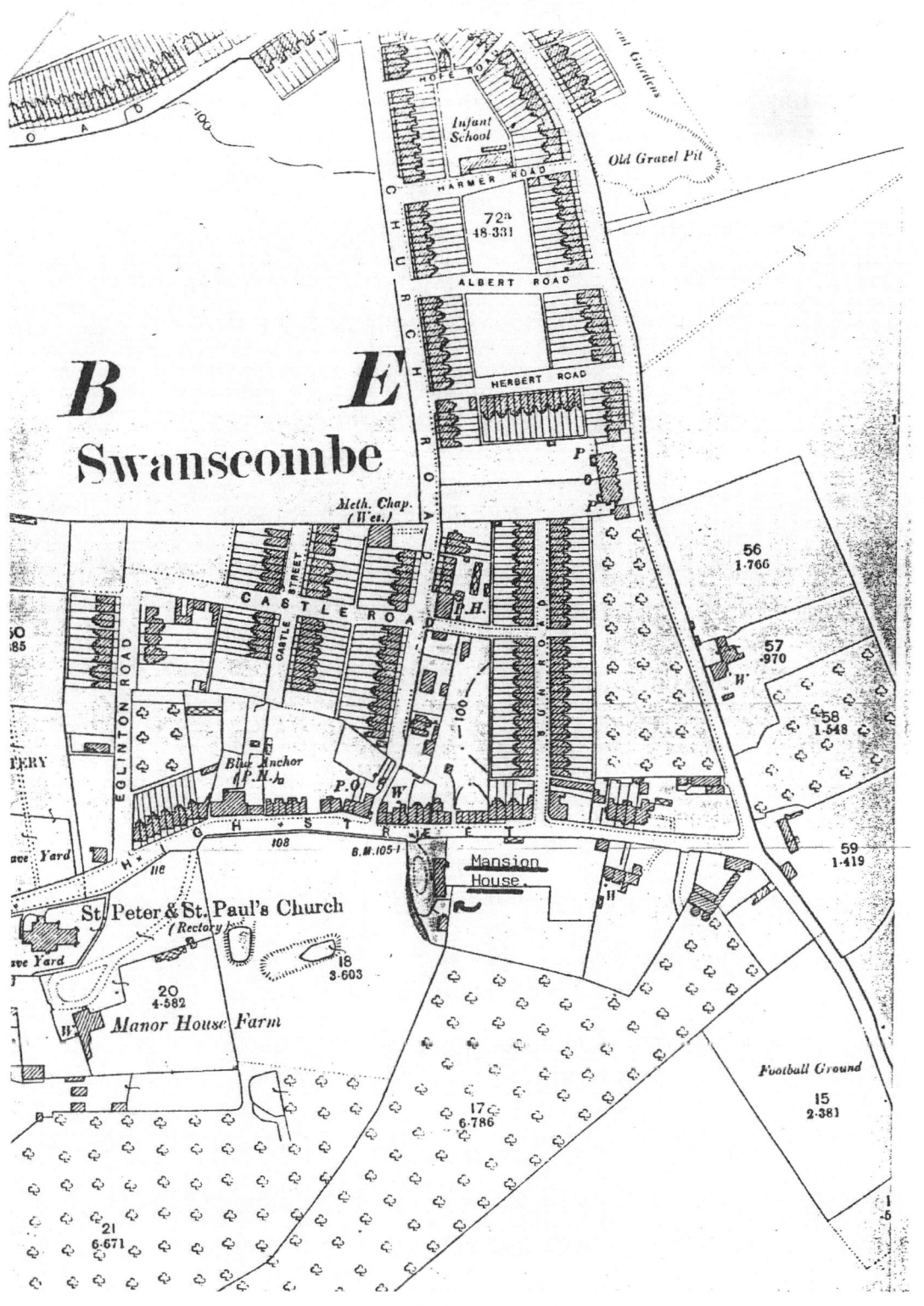

Contents

Chapter 1
Suinescamp – Swanscombe
Introduction to Swanscombe's landscape, history and development of local government.

Chapter 2
Edward Hasted's The History and Topographical Survey of the County of Kent: Swanscombe: Volume 2 (1797)

Chapter 3
St Peter & Paul Church 1050-Present & All Saints Church Galley Hill 1894-1997

Chapter 4
White Works Cement Industry 1825-1990

Chapter 5
Galley Hill Man 1888 & Swanscombe Woman 1935

Chapter 6
Places and Buildings to Remember

Chapter 7
Transport Trams and Trains

Chapter 8
Beer & Public Houses

Chapter 9
A Walk Round Swanscombe

Chapter 10
War Years

Chapter 11
Schools & Education

Chapter 12
Swanscombe Football

Chapter 13
Adverts

Chapter 14
Other Photographs
Future Developments

Chapter 1

Suinescamp – Swanscombe

Introductions by Christoph Bull

Domesday Book Swanscombe Paragraph

INTRODUCTION

The ancient parish of **Swanscombe**, whose boundaries are those of the present town council, encompasses 2142 acres, or 3.34 square miles.

To the north is the River Thames; to the east the Ebbsfleet Stream, which separates **Swanscombe** from Northfleet. Watling Street, now the A2, forms Swanscombe's southern boundary with Southfleet while Bean Road/Cobham Terrace and the Station Road area at Greenhithe mark the western border with Stone.

The geology of **Swanscombe** consists of alluvium on the marshes to the north stretching down the Ebbsfleet Valley along the Northfleet boundary to Springhead. An area of upper chalk follows which covers the area of the former cement works, the industrial estate bordering Northfleet and most of the site of Baker's Hole to the east of **Swanscombe** village. Much of the Galley Hill, Milton Road and Ames Road area is standing on an outcrop of Boyn Hill Terrace gravel. **Swanscombe** Street and the church of St Peter and St Paul sit on Thanet sand, as does Alkerden Farm. The area of **Swanscombe** Woods, now mostly destroyed by quarries, was originally Blackheath and Woolwich beds of sand, pebbles, clays and loams with a large outcrop of London clay in the centre, which stretched down to Watling Street.

Within the geological landscape the land rises in height from a few feet above sea level on the northern marshes to 250 feet in the extreme south of the parish.

Until the mid 19th century, **Swanscombe** was a parish of two main settlements: Greenhithe in the west by the Thames, and **Swanscombe** Street, roughly east of centre, which was the home of the church and manor house. Small hamlets at Galley Hill, Knockhall, Milton Street and Western Cross, completed the pattern of settlements, except for a few farms dotted about, such as Alkerden, New Barn and Western Cross. The settlement at Greenhithe, which has its own article (under history, in the Greenhithe section of the web site), will be largely ignored in this article. Each farm, village and hamlet had orchards associated with it, while two large wooded areas existed at Mounts Wood (south of Greenhithe) and **Swanscombe** Wood (known as **Swanscombe** Park) to the south of **Swanscombe** village itself. Road communications were mainly via the London Road running along a position north of **Swanscombe** and south of Greenhithe; the basic road system has changed little since the 19th century.

Until the early years of this century many associated Swanscombe's name with "Sweyne's Camp" – the site of the Viking invaders' settlement during the raids of the 830s AD. Wallenberg suggests the name derives from Old English "swan" (or "swineherd") and "camp" (or "field").

The Domesday Book

Introduction: Landscape of Swanscombe

The single most important historical and technological influence on the landscape of the whole area is that of cement manufacture and the consequent tortured landscape left after the excavation of chalk, clay and gravel.

Swanscombe ancient parish (which includes Greenhithe) consists of extensive marshes in the northeast stretching out into the Thames – the river forming the district's northern boundary. The marshes form a peninsular known as Broadness or Swanssombe marshes, and this area is split into two thirds being in Swanscombe and one third in Northfleet – Swanscombe eastern neighbour.

The marshes form an extremely valuable part of the area not only as a flood plain but also as an open space with footpaths crossing the peninsula with the ability for the public to reach the shore of the Thames. This area was largely denied easy access to local residents since the blocking up the ancient footpath known as Pilgrims Road which leads directly from Swanscombe's Galley Hill area down onto the marshes. Part of the route of the Channel Tunnel Rail Link runs across the southern end of the marshes. In February 2010, after a campaign by Swanscombe & Greenhithe Town Council, with evidence given by Christoph Bull and others, Pilgrims Road ancient right of way was reopened.

The North West part of the district is Greenhithe – a very interesting maritime village directly on the river's edge and associated with Ingress Abbey and the surrounding parkland. Here the chalk goes right up to the river bank with no marshes separating Greenhithe from the river – opposite to the Swanscombe.

The major area covered with housing stretches from Greenhithe south to Knockhall and then east meeting up with Swanscombe, although the two are separated by chalk pits.

The South of the Swanscombe-Greenhithe development is now known as "Eastern Quarry" but was once farmland and the site of the Mounts and Swanscombe Woods. The huge quarry, which was created by the cement industry has ceased production of chalk and other materials (in 2008) and will be home to five new urban villages as part of the Kent Thameside development, of which Swanscombe and Greenhithe form the heart

 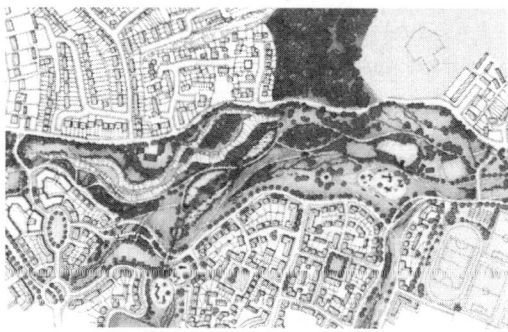

The above pictures show eastern quarry as it is now and the proposed development which is planned.

The eastern area of Swanscombe is the Ebbsfleet stream which forms the boundary with Northfleet – a large part of this area is reclaimed chalk pits (the northern one is known as "Bakers Hole").

Finally Swanscombe's Southern boundary is the ancient Watling Street, now the A2 beyond which is the predominately rural area of Southfleet.

Swanscombe and Greenhithe is largely a post industrial landscape and its older built up areas show this clearly with streets of workers cottages – in some ways the town has more in common with coal mining communities rather than the typical Kentish settlements. Greenhithe, on the other hand, is quite different – it is a riverside community but also has the legacy of the cement industry surround it – despoiled land and old worked out pits.

Swanscombe

Swanscombe is without question the most important archaeological site for prehistoric remains in Kent if not the whole of the country. An accident of local geology, coupled with cement needing to extract materials from the ground, means that so much has been uncovered. The famous Swanscombe Skull was discovered in Barnfield Pit off Craylands Lane in 3 fragments in 1935, 1936 and 1955, is now thought to be around 400,000 years old. The whole Barnfield Pit site is one of outstanding scientific and historical interest – and since 2005 it has been known as the Swanscombe Heritage Park which has displays and panels and walks to explain the importance of the area. As a direct result of Swanscombe's richness in such human and animal remains, Henry Stopes (died in 1902 and buried in Swanscombe Cemetery) rented a house here with his family – including his now famous daughter Marie Stopes (1880-1958) the pioneer in family planning.

Another important Kentish figure who lived at Swanscombe was Sir Anthony Weldon (died 1648). Sir Anthony was the powerful leader of Kentish government during the Civil Wars as Chairman of the Parliamentarian County Committee – he managed to abolish Christmas in 1648 and he also made Rochester Castle a ruin after selling of the roof and floor timbers!

Until the 19th Century Swanscombe was a small agricultural village along what is now Swanscombe Street – the current built up High Street was then merely a country lane leading to the village.

In 1825 Swanscombe Cement Works opened on the edge of the marshes and over the next 100 years came to dominate the whole parish, defying an attempt to close it in the 1870s and eventually buying up the Manor of Swanscombe in 1872. The chance of employments for unskilled men was a great draw and so between 1801 and 1911 the population grew by over 900% changing a small village into a small industrial town.

The former country lane became the High Street and other streets grew up around Galley Hill, which eventually led to the whole area from Milton Street to Galley Hill to Swanscombe village becoming one joined up area of development. This huge change in population and growth brought with it many problems with over crowding poor sanitary conditions and water supply – and this needed to be tackled by local government rather than leaving everything to the cement factory owners and private speculators.

The cement industry brought population and with population came shop keepers, service industries and numerous public houses and beer houses as well as Gallery Hill Church (All Saints which was originally opened in 1881 – the current church, which has been converted into flats since 1990, was opened in July 1895) and literary institutes, clubs and societies and libraries were created to provide wholesome entertainment the workers.

The character of Swanscombe can be clearly seen today in the roads filled with terrace houses built to house the ever growing industrial population – former farm houses were demolished and lost their land to cement and clay extraction. Swanscombe Cement works closed in 1990.

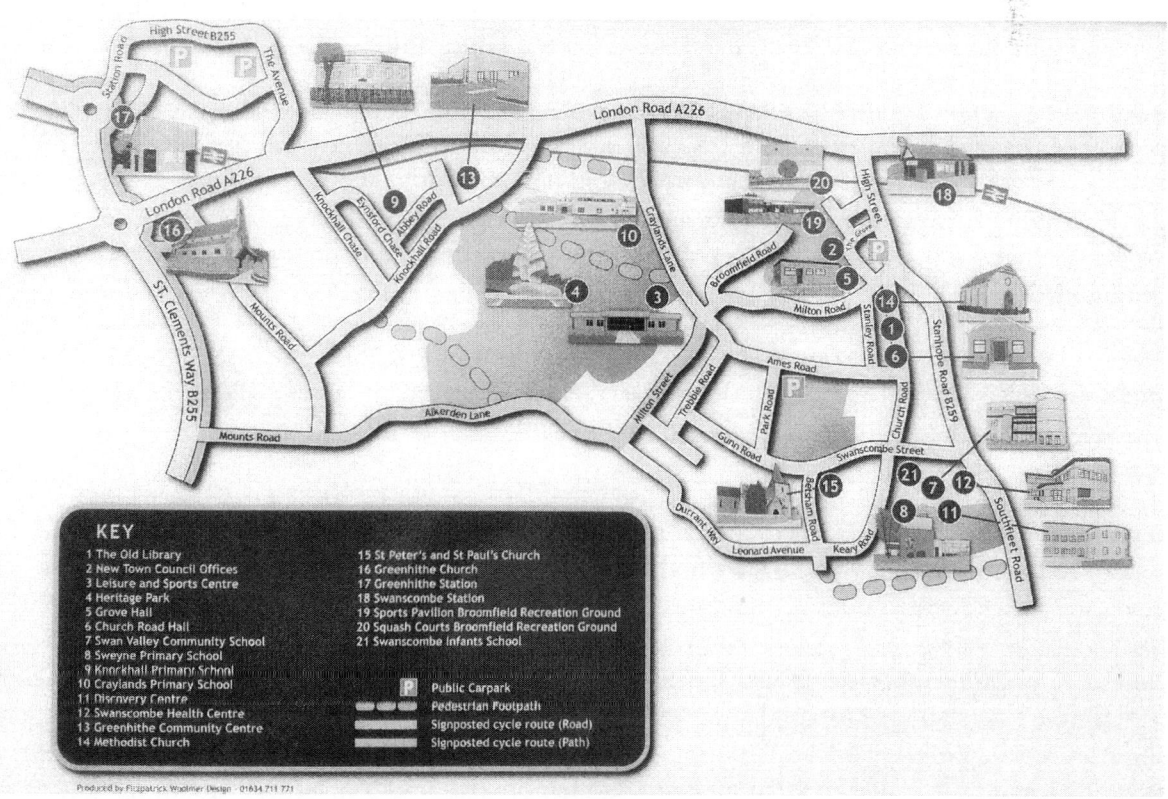

Information map of Swanscombe

Swanscombe and Greenhithe Local Government

It is a fact that in Victorian times, just as it is today, that the only thing that stands between order and civilization on one hand, and chaos on the other, is local government.

In 1894, local councils were set up to deal with daily problems that the churches and small cliques of the past were overwhelmed by.

Swanscombe, although steadily growing and producing ever more money in rates because of the factories and the workers to go with them, was forced to become a parish council under the Dartford Rural District, which covered a large area from Swanscombe to West Kingsdown and from Swanley to Southfleet.

Swanscombe's first meeting was at Ingress Vale Chapel in Knockhall Road on 4th December 1894. Walter Ames was elected chairman (he also became the first chairman of Swanscombe Urban District in 1926 and Ames Road is named after him). Right from the first Swanscombe resented being part of a rural areas and was pushing for more powers and independence. At this very first meeting 15 councilor's were elected from a list of 35 candidates. In 1898, a fire brigade was created – with help from Northfleet Urban District Council who already had an organized fire brigade. From 1894 until 1902, the parish council met in Galley Hill School, which stood on the north side of London Road. In 1902 until 1922, the council met in Galley Hill Church House, which was opposite the George & Dragon public house and had been the original Galley Hill Church before 1895.

The most important symbol of Swanscombe's growing confidence and wish for independence came in 1908 when the parish council paid for Swanscombe Fire Station to be built in Church Road – it was the first structure to be built and owned by the council. The idea was to build another storey on top of the single storey fire station for a council chamber and offices, but this was not done until 1922 when A.E Frost, the building and undertakers of Swanscombe, won the contract to extend the original fire station building.

Meanwhile, Swanscombe's councilor's were complaining about having to attend meetings miles away from home to suit the huge Dartford Rural District, and that as the biggest and richest parish, they still only had the same voting rights as tiny places like Ridley and Lullingstone.

It was during the early years of the 20th Century that Rev. Stanley Morgan became a councilor. Morgan was the minister at the congregational chapel in Greenhithe and he was a Christian-Socialist. Morgan remembered many years later that his early experience of the most dreadful poverty and want among the villagers of Greenhithe and the workers of Swanscombe, had pushed him into taking action via local government. Stanley Morgan was several times chairman of Swanscombe council until his death in 1951 (indeed his record as chairman is unbeaten to this day. He was chairman of the parish council nine times and the urban district council five times). Linked to Morgan's own views and supported by men of very different political outlooks, such as the Moore Family who were important councilor's and owners of the mineral water and lemonade factory in Milton Road, was the ever louder demand to leave Dartford Rural District and become their own council with power to make a difference in Swanscombe and Greenhithe. In 1923, Swanscombe Parish Council began a campaign, which resulted in it becoming an Urban District Council in 1926 and so leaving Dartford Rural to be master of its own resources. Dartford Rural District fought this proposal until it was obvious that Swanscombe had the support of Kent County Council for going it alone.

The new Swanscombe Urban District Council immediately moved from above the Fire Station to a house at Swanscombe Cross (entrance to the cement works) where it rented what had been the cement factory's owners dwelling.

Swanscombe Urban District Council then set about buildings "A better and Brighter Swanscombe" including the Recreation Ground (1932), swimming baths in London Road (1936), improved council housing (1926 to the 1970's), extending sewerage to decrease use in cesspools (1926 onwards) and to help Kent County Library establish one of the first libraries with paid staff in the former council chamber over the Fire Station (1928-9). (see page 102)

In the 1940's, Swanscombe Urban District Council wanted to move to Knockhall Lodge, a large Victorian house in Knockhall Road, but although it purchased the house, the property had become so dilapidated during World War II that it was subsequently sold and demolished.

In 1964, the Manor Farm House in Swanscombe Street was bought and this lovely 18th century building was destroyed and replaced with a soulless office, which was itself demolished in 1989. (See pages 103).

The Local Government Reorganisation, which came into effect in 1974, undid all the work and effort of Swanscombe and Greenhithe's civic fathers in the early 20th century – urban districts councils were abolished and Swanscombe was returned to being a parish council under a new Dartford District. This caused a great deal of resentment in Swanscombe with councilor's no longer having any real power over their community and not helped by their facilities being sold off from under them such as the swimming pool in London Road.

In 1989, the Swanscombe Centre was opened in Craylands Lane – as sports, social and local government facility – and this became the home of Swanscombe and Greenhithe Town Council until 2007. The new facility was not welcomed because the councilor's did not want to lose their ugly but purpose built headquarters, which they had built with Swanscombe's own money – the new centre was also very cramped for council meetings.

The brand new and present council offices, on two storeys in The Grove was opened in 2007 and gives far more room and facilities – and is a pleasing piece of architecture. Swanscombe and Greenhithe are entering a huge time of change, as the Kent Thameside development is about to cover the Eastern Quarry with houses the development around the newly opened Ebbsfleet International Railway Station (November 2007) and possible development on the flood plain on Swanscombe Marshes, the town council's need for more facilities is pressing. The present time of development is already changing the nature of Swanscombe – the working class industrial era replaced a rural one. The current post industrial society is being diluted by non locals and those developments which are bringing a different people with different aspirations – in an increasingly different world

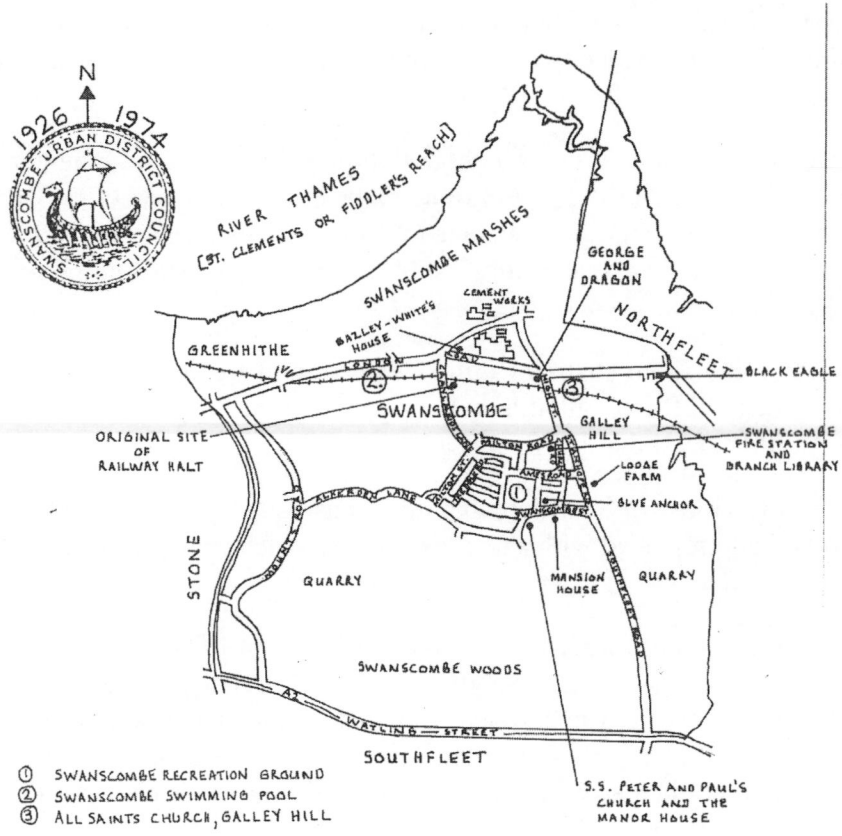

Map courtesy of Christoph Bull and Georgie Hammond

*Official Opening
Of
Council Offices
Manor House
26th September 1964*

Chapter 2

The History and Topographical Survey of the County of Kent: Swanscombe: Volume 2 (1797) by Edward Hasted

Edward Hasted (1732-1812) was the author of Kent's greatest single history – all researched and written during the eighteenth century without the benefit of new technology and when many archives and libraries were not open to the public. The entire work was divided into a dozen volumes and was arranged by the local parish within Kent's organization of provinces (known as "lathes" – of which Swanscombe formed part of the Lathe of Sutton at Hone) and then the subdivision of the lathes (known as "Hundreds", Swanscombe was part of Axstane Hundred).

Typical of its time, Hasted's work was designed to be of interest to those who would be able to support his massive project financially – in other words the landowners – it is not like modern local histories which are overwhelmingly based on the life ordinary people. The extract below is from the second edition 1797 and as you will see there is little about the people who were not landowners, rectors or major benefactors of the parish – and virtually nothing about the buildings other than the large houses and Manors.

Christoph Bull

The History and Topographical Survey of the County of Kent: Volume 2 (1797)

SWANSCOMBE.

EASTWARD from Stone lies Swanscombe, so called from the camp of Swane, king of Denmark, who having sailed up the Thames, landed at Greenhithe; and marching from thence, encamped at this place; Combe and Compe in Saxon, being derived from *campus* in Latin, signifying a camp. (fn. 1)

It is written in some records *Swegenscomp, Swaneskampe,* (fn. 2) and in Domesday *Suinescamp.*

The high road from London to Dover crosses the northern part of this parish, which reaches up higher a long way to the southward, among a large tract of woodland. It contains in the whole 2300 acres of land, of which 600 are wood, and 250 marsh land. On the north side of the above road there is a large range of chalk pits, and lower down the hamlet of Greenhithe, (called in the *Textus Roffensis, Gretenersce* (fn. 3)) close to the shore of the river Thames. Here there are several wharfs for the landing and shipping of corn, wood, coals, and other commodities, but the greatest traffic arises from the chalk and lime, from the above chalk pits, the range of which continues with small intermission from Stone to Gravesend, within a very small distance of the shore. Hence not only the city of London, but the adjacent counties, and even those of Suffolk and Norfolk, are supplied with this commodity. There is a ferry here across the Thames into Essex, for horses and cattle only, which antiently belonged to the priory of Dartford; at the suppression of which, in king Henry the VIIIth's reign, it was granted to John Bere for a term of years, (fn. 4) and afterwards by queen Elizabeth in her 2d year, with the manor of Swanscombe to Anthony Weldon, in fee, since which it has continued with the possessors of the manor to the present time.

There was a chapel formerly in this hamlet, founded by John Lucas, of Greenhithe, who, in the 19th year of king Edward the IIId. Obtained the king's licence to assign over a piece of ground here, and twenty acres of pasture in this parish, to a chaplain, to celebrate divine offices daily in the chapel, to be erected on it here, in honor of the blessed Virgin Mary. This chapel was suppressed with others of the same sort in king Edward the Vith's reign, some of the walls of it are re maining, but being converted into a tenement, there is scarce any outward appearance of it left.

At the east end of this hamlet is the seat of Ingress, situated close under the chalk cliffs, on the bank of the Thames, along which it has a most pleasing view, the extensive pleasure grounds of it are for the most part formed over the remains of a range of old neglected chalk pits, which form an inequality of ground for the purpose, beyond what any art or present expence could perhaps easily attain to. Above the London road, on the southern side, is a neat modern house, called Knockholt, built by one of the family of Hayes, of Cobham, the last of whom Mr. Bonham Hayes left it by will to Mr. Butler, of Deal, who now owns it; near it are two small hamlets, called Milton-street and Weston-cross.

From the above road the ground rises southward to the village of Swanscombe, at the west end of which is the mansion of the manor, much of which has within these few years been pulled down, and it is now used as a farm house; and a little further the parsonage and church. Round the village there is some tolerable good land, though rather inclined to gravel, and some orchard ground; even so early as the 36th year of king Henry VIII. Mention is made in a grant of it of an orchard here, called the cherry-garden, belonging to the mansion of the manor. Above the village the ground rises still higher, being covered with a large tract of woodland, the soil of which is a stiff cold clay. These woods stop the current of the air, and occasion the fogs and noisome vapours arising from the marshes to hang among them, and then to descend on the village and low lands again, which renders this parish exceedingly unhealthy. Part of these woods within the bounds of this parish is known by the name of Swanscombe park, in which and other parts near it there are several mounts of earth thrown up, seemingly the works of very antient times. They all lie very high, some of them have a hollow at the top, and none of them are above thirty or forty yards over. The old Roman road runs along the southern part of this wood. Dr. Thorpe supposed that Swanscombe was the *vagniace* of the Romans, and that their station here was at the head of the fleet, which parts this parish and Northfleet, on which subject the reader will find further hereafter under Southfleet. A few years ago a copper coin of Nero was grubbed up out of a hedgerow in this parish, and another of Severus was turned up by the plough; a sussicient corroboration that the Romans had intercourse in or near this place.

William the Conqueror, as is commonly reported, was met in his way through this county, immediately after the battle of Hastings, by the Kentishmen at Swanscombe, headed by archbishop Stigand, and Egelsine, the abbot of St. Augustines, each man having a bough in his hand; so that the whole multitude seemed at first a moving forest; when throwing down their boughs, at the sound of the trumpet, they appeared with their arms prepared for battle. This at first somewhat alarmed the duke, but his 16hannele ceased, when he found it was the people of Kent, who, as he was told, by the archbishop and abbot, were come to assure him of the submission of the county, and withal to demand the confirmation of their antient laws and privileges. The duke received them very graciously, and not so willingly, as wisely, granted their request.

This tale is repeated by William Thorne, monk of St. Augustine's, Canterbury, from a MSS. History of that abbey, drawn up by Thomas Sport, and others, chroniclers there, who in all probability invented it, to magnify the valour of their archbishop and abbot, and of their countrymen. All our writers, except Mr. Lambarde, who seems loth to give it up, have looked upon this story as a mere fiction. Mr. Somner, in particular, calls it a *commentitious sable*; he says, it is mentioned only by Sprot, who lived in the reign of king Edward I. and such others as of latter times have written after his copy; for before him, and in that interim of more than two hundred years, between the conquest and the time he wrote, no published story, no chronicle, no record of any kind, Kentish or other, is found to warrant the relation; and yet, a matter so remarkable as this, was not likely to escape all our historians pens that were before him, especially those about the time of the conquest. Among which the silence of Ingulphus is the more strange, since he is so particular and punctual in relating and recording the Conqueror's oppugners and their proceedings. These reasons, with others, he offers to the more literate and judicious only, for the story being so universally swallowed by the generality of people, he dares not enter into a dispute with them about it, as despairing of success in disengaging them from the belief of it, though he was to use the most convincing arguments for that purpose. (fn. 5)

Our herbalists have taken notice of the following SCARCE HERBS and PLANTS to be found within this parish:

In the reign of king William the Conqueror, Swanscombe was part of the possessions of Odo, bishop of Baieux, the king's half brother, and it is accordingly entered, under the general title of his lands, in the survey of Domesday, as follows:

Helto holds Sninescamp of the bishop (of Baieux.) It was taxed at 10 sulings. The arable land is 14 carucates. There are 3 in demesne, and 33 villeins, with 3 borderers, having 13 carucates. There is 1 knight, and 10 servants, and 40 acres of meadow, wood for three hogs and 5 fisheries of 30 pence, and a sixth which belongs to the hall, and 1 hith of 5 shillings and 4 pence; of the wood of this manor, Richard (de Tunbridge) holds in his lowy as much as is worth 4 shilling.

The whole manor was worth 20 pounds .... and it is now worth 32 pounds.

On the disgrace of bishop Odo, in 1084, his possessions were consiscated to the king's use, and this manor as part of them. After which the manor of Swanscombe came into the possession of the family of Montchensie, called in Latin *De Monte Canisio*.

The manor of Swanscombe, as well as that of Combe in this parish, holden of Rochester-castle, owed service towards the defence of it, the owner of Swanscombe being, as it were, one of the principal captains to whom that charge was antiently committed, and there were subject to this manor several knights sees, as petty or subordinate captains, bound to serve under his banner there. (fn. 22)

These services have been long since turned into annual rents of money. The following is a list of those manors and lands which held by *castle-guard*, and now pay rents in lieu of it:

Luddesdown manor. Ryarsh manor. Delce Magna. Addington manor. Norton manor. Cobham Eastcourt, and Aldington Eastcourt. Stockbury manor. Little Delce. Hamwold-court manor. Farnborough-court manor. Boughton Monchelsea manor. Midley and Little Caldecott. Goddington manor. Padlesworth manor. Bicknor manor. Fraxingham manor. Wootton manor.

Eccles manor. Part of ditto. Sholden manor in Surry. Lands in Westborough farm, in Surry. Dairy farm, in Higham. Mickleham manor, in Surry. Barrow-hall manor, in ditto. Ingrast, Harringfield, East Harringfield, and West Horden, in Essex. Great and Little Borstable manors. Widford manor, in Essex. Alchardin, alias Combes manor, and part of North-court.

These rents are paid on St. Andrew's day, old style, and the custom has been held, that if the rent is not then paid, it is liable to be doubled, on the return of every tide in the Medway, during the time it remains unpaid. This custom was very near being brought to a legal decision some years ago; for Sir Thomas Dyke, bart. Owner of Farnborough-court manor, and Thomas Best, esq. owner of Eccles manor, having made default in the payment of their castle-guard rents, Mr. Child, owner of Swanscombe manor, and the castle, required the penalty of their being doubled; which dispute was carried so far, that ejectments were served on the estates, and a special jury was struck, to try the matter. But by the interposition of friends, the dispute was compromised, and a small composition was accepted, in lieu of the penalty, though it was entered in the court-rolls of Swanscombe manor, with the consent of all parties, in such a manner, that the custom of this payment might not be lessened in future by it.

Charities.

Martin MERIEL, of Greenhithe, by his will in 1563, devised 20s. yearly, to be paid out of his house and lands, called Daniel's, in Swanscombe, to be applied, 18s. towards the relief of the poor of this parish, on Good Friday, and 2s. to the churchwardens, in consideration of their pains.

John BERE, gent. In the reign of queen Elizabeth, by will, appointed that James Vaughan and others, and their heirs, enfeoffed by him by deed, in three tenements and gardens, situated in Greenhithe, should stand seised of them, for the purpose, that three aged poor men or women should for ever be placed in them, by the clergymen and churchwardens, they being inhabitants, and to enjoy the same *gratis* during their lives.

Anthony POULTER, as is supposed, gave by will, in 1635, 20s. yearly, to be distributed by the churchwardens to the poor, at Christmas, which money is paid by Mrs. A. Pettit, of Dartford.

Lady SWAN gave, by will, in 1721, three messuages in Greenhithe, to the churchwardens and overseers, the yearly rents of them, to be distributed among the poorest inhabitants of this parish as they should think fit, or to permit so many such to dwell in them *gratis*, the same now vested in the churchwardens; a part of the premises was let to the late Mr. Richard Forrest, for ninety-nine years, and occupied by him at 3l. per annum; another small part is in the occupation of James King, at 5s. per annum, and the remainder is turned into a workhouse.

ONE PIECE of land, called the Poor Acre, and other lands belonging to B. Hayes, esq. pays 1l. 5s. to the churchwardens, for the use of the poor of the parish yearly, the donor unknown.

SWANSCOMBE is within the ECCLESIASTICAL JURISDICTION of the *diocese* and *deanry* of Rochester. This church, which is dedicated to St. Peter and St. Paul, consists of two isles and two chancels, having a spire steeple at the west end.

In this church, among other monuments and inscriptions, are the following. *In the isle*, are several gravestones, with memorials, for the Tuckeys, Acortes, Wallis's, and other inhabitants, of this parish. A mural monument, on the north isle, for Mr. John Sloman, obt. 1706, æt. 21, only surviving son of Mr. Anthony Sloman, of London; he left his fortune to his sole executor, Mr. Jonathan Smith, younger son of John Smith, esq. (his grandfather by his mother's side) by a second marriage. *In the great chancel*, a memorial for the wife of Anthony Weldon, esq. obt. 1759; above these arms, a cinquefoil, on a chief a demi lion. Another within the rails, for the Rev. John Watts, obt. Jan. 12, 1670. A memorial for John Taylor, clerk, B. D. rector of this parish, obt. Sep. 2, 1757, æt. 60, arms, ermine on a chief indented, three escallop shells, impaling a chevron ermine between three garles. Another for Martin Barnes, B. D. rector of this parish, ob. Sep. 27, 1759, æt. 59. On the south side a mural monument, with the figure of a woman finely executed, and kneeling at a desk, with a book open before her, and an inscription for dame Ellinor Weldon, daughter of George Wilmer, esq. and wife of Sir Anthony Weldon, by whom he had six sons and four daughters living, obt. 1622. On the south side of the rails, a mural monument, with a like figure of a man, kneeling at a desk, with a book open before him, and inscription, for Anthony Weldon, who died, clerk of the greencloth to queen Elizabeth, and brother of Sir Ralph Weldon, who died in the same office to king James I. himself being clerk of the kitchen both to queen Elizabeth and king James I. who resigned the same place to his nephew, Anthony Weldon, then clerk of the kitchen, in the 2d year of that king's reign, obt. 1613, arms, Weldon. *In the south chancel*, a monument for Elianor, relict of Wm. Say, esq. ob. 1678; above, a shield with three chevrons, impaling Weldon. Another for Elizabeth, relict of Wm. Hart, esq. obt. 1677; above, these arms, a lozenge, Hart, impaling Weldon; another for Anne, relict of Sir Percival Hart, of Lullingstone, obt. 1712. A memorial, at the east end of the south chancel, for Thomas Blechinden, esq. lord of this manor, obt. 1740, æt. 31, and for his widow, Mrs. Lidia Blechingdon, obt. 1743, æt. 31; above are these arms, quarterly, 1st and 4th, a fess 17hannel between three lions heads erased; 2d and 3d, a chevron between three eagles heads erased, impaling a fess ermine between three cinquesoils. At the upper end of the south side, a stately monument of alabaster, on which are the figures of a knight in armour and his lady, at large, resting on pillows, at his feet a son cumbent, and at her's, a daughter; and in front, under two tablets, are three sons and five daughters, kneeling, in the dress of the age; between them is a desk, with a book open on each side, being for Sir Ralph Weldon, erected by his wife, lady Elizabeth Weldon; he was chief clerk of the kitchen to queen Elizabeth, afterwards clerk comptroller to king James, and died clerk of the green cloth, an. 1609, having had by the said Elizabeth, daughter of Leven Buffkin, esq. four sons; Anthony, clerk of the kitchen to king James, Henry, Lever, and Ralph; and six daughters. On another tablet, an inscription, shewing that his grandfather, Edw. Weldon, served king Henry VII. And was master of the household to king Henry VIII. Whom likewise Thomas Weldon, his uncle, served, and was cofferer to king Edward VI. And queen Elizabeth; Anthony Weldon, his father, served queen Elizabeth, and died clerk of the Greencloth; on the top, these arms, quarterly, 1st and 4th, Weldon; 2d, ermine, a lion rampant, his tail forked azure, crowned or; 3d, argent, on a chevron azure, three besants between three trefoils, parted per pale gules and vert; on the left side a shield, being Weldon, impaling on a bend ermine, three boars heads couped, between two bendlets or; on the right, Weldon, impaling Buffkin. In the upper window of the south chancel are these arms, very antient, in coloured glass, 1st quarterly, 1st and 4th, argent, a chevron between three rooks proper; 2d and 3d, per pale indented, quarterly and azure, a lion rampant or, impaling chequy or and azure, a fess gules. (fn. 27)

This church, in former times, was much resorted to by a company of pilgrims, who came hither for St. Hildeserth's help, who by his picture, which was in the upper window of the south side, appears to have been a bishop, to whom such as were distracted came to be cured of their infanity. (fn. 28)

From the earliest account of time it was esteemed an appendage to the manor of Swanscombe; although, in the reign of king Henry III. There arose a dispute between the prior and convent of St. Mary's, in Southwark, and Warine de Monchensie, concerning the advowson and right of presentation to it; but the prior and convent allowed it to belong to Warine de Monchensie, saving to the prior and his successors, the annual sum of five marcs sterling, to be paid by the rector of it. (fn. 29)

The church continued appendant to the manor till Edward VI. Dec. 4, in his 6th year, granted the advowson of the rectory of it, with other premises, in exchange, to Edward lord Clinton and Say, and Henry Herdson. (fn. 30)

In king James I.'s reign, the advowson belonged to Mr. George Gardiner. In 1650, it was the property of the Rev. Mr. Betts, who was likewise rector of this church. It has been, for many years past, part of the possessions of the master and fellows of Sidney college in Cambridge, the present proprietors of it.

In the 15th year of king Edward I. the rectory of Swanscombe was valued at thirty marcs. (fn. 31)

By virtue of the *commission of enquiry* into the value of church livings, in 1650, it was returned, that Swanscombe was a parsonage, with a house, and about twenty acres of glebe land, all worth 120l. per annum, master Betts enjoying the same, who had the advowson. (fn. 32) About which time there was a suit between the lord of the manor and the rector of this parish, relating to tithes, which was determined in the exchequer in favour of the latter, of which there is a curious memorandum inserted in the Register.

It is valued in the king's books at 25l. 13s. 4d. and the yearly tenths at 2l. 11s. 4d. (fn. 33)

Chapter 3

St Peter & Paul Church
1050 – Present
All Saints Church Galley Hill
1894 – 1990

The Church of St.Peter and St.Paul 1050-Present

Swanscombe Church 1803

Introduction:

Swanscombe, between Dartford and Gravesend, is one of the North Kent's great cement making centres and, indeed, this noted industry has been carried on since Tudor and Stuart times. Though much of the town has a workaday aspect the corner around the parish church still preserves a rural charm and into this setting the church is one of the most interesting in North Kent with its very fine Saxon tower and its wealth of interesting memorials and tombs. Its stones tell the story of Swanscombe through the ages

History

According to the early records Swanscombe takes its name from Sweyne's Camp, as such its manor was recorded in the Domesday Survey. The camp was in fact a winter camp set up by Sweyne, a Danish King, to protect his fleet, In those days, of course, the Kent coast was constantly being raided by Danish troops. The Local inhabitants lived in constant fear of being plundered and possibly being kidnapped as slaves.

Swanscombe had, however, been inhaboted long before the days of the Danes, That area was occupied in prehistoric times is shown by the fact that a 50,000 year old skull was found in Swanscombe

The first church on the present site was built in the 6th century but was destroyed by the Danes, and would have been most likely made from wood and some stone. In the more peaceful era of King Canute the church was rebuilt and of the Saxon period a few reminders are found in the present church consisted only of a nave with a rough form of tower. Its exact date cannot be accurately placed but it was not likely to have been before 1050 (900th anniversary kept in 1953).

Its is said that after the Battle of Hastings, William the Conqueror returned to London through North Kent and at Swanscombe was halted by a "moving forest". In fact it was a local army each carrying a bough from a leafy tree. This array so impressed the King that he gave permission to the Men of Kent to return their ancient right of gavel-kind a law which divides a dead landowner's estate equally among his sons.

The Normans enlarged the church though they did not completely eliminate the work of the Saxons. They added a chancel to the nave and built a sturdier tower. In the 13th Century – Early English period the nave was largely rebuilt in that style of architecture. The first incumbent was appointed in 1320.

After the Norman period the manor of Swanscombe passed through various hands. The de Valence and Mortimer families owned it and then in later years it was given by Queen Elizabeth I to the Weldons. From that family it passed to the Childs and was later acquired by the Earl of Jersey.

In the latter part of the mediaeval period the time of the Tudors and Stuarts, Swanscombe assumed something of its industrial character as cement working and lime burning began to become important.

A Picture of the Swanscombe of the 19th century is given in a Gazetteer of 1866. This tells us that the place was a parish of 2,593 acres of which one fifth was water. There were 414 Houses and a population of 2,323 and this included Greenhithe. The report concludes "The manor house is an ancient building now occupied by J Coveney Esq. Swanscombe Wood is a famous rural retreat, frequented by gypsying parties and contains a cavern called Clappernappers Hole, associated with mush curious legend.

The living is a rectory in the diocese of Rochester, Value £600. Patron Sidney Sussex College, Cambridge. There are almshouses and other charities of £23.

In 1873-4 the church was Thoroughly restored and the main north porch was rebuilt the expense being borne by the brethren of the Erasmus Wilson F.R.S.

The Fire

On August the 14th 1902, the church was struck by lighting and the resulting fire caused a great deal of damage mostly in the nave. Restorations were at once put in hand. The funds were donated by fund raising and by donations.

Drawing of the fire 1902

Internal Postcard of the Fire Damage 1902

Newspaper Photograph of the clean up 1902

The Destruction of Swanscombe Church

(An Account of the fire in <u>The Gravesend Standard</u> 23rd Aug 1902)

Swanscombe Parish Church SS.Peter and Paul, was struck by lightning during a thunderstorm which raged over the district on 14th Aug 1902 Thursday afternoon, at about five o'clock q terribly vivid flash struck the, it is said, the lower part of the lighting rod had failed to earth, and conveyed the lightning into to church, where upon caught some of the fine old woodwork close to the porch. Soon the whole of the interior was on fire. The Swanscombe fire brigade were called, and were on the scene in ten minutes. Meanwhile a crowd had gathered to watch the horror of their beloved church burn in front of them helpless to do anything about it. The church presented a terrible sight, the lurid red and orange glow of the flames seen coming through the windows was a sight they felt they would never live to see.

Despite their prompt response to the call, the fire brigade were almost powerless, for the flames had attained such a hold on the building that the damage to the tower and entrance had all but been demolished. Dispatching urgent called to the Northfleet and Gravesend Brigades to assist. The Swanscombe Men has little choice to saving what they could. So they set about saving the chancel, and the valuable pictures and tapestries were brought out. The communion plate was also brought out from the vestry, and a number of Bibles and Prayer Books were rescued. As for the parish registers, these were placed in a fire proof safe under the flooring, and it was felt that they should be safe. In any case a rescue would have been fool hardy. The Northfleet Fire brigade arrived, having been called at six o'clock, the Northfleet Brewery Company having kindly supplied horses. The Brigade under Capt. Boucher, also directed all of their efforts to the saving of the chancel.

The supply of water was totally inadequate, and the nearest hydrant, opposite the "Blue Anchor" Inn was accidentally broken off. There was however a pond at the back of the church, and the hand engine was sent there. The nearest hydrant was now 300 to 350 yards away, and the brigades connected this. But even then the firemen found it difficult to lift the water high enough.

They eyes of the crowd were now riveted to the steeple a structure of tiles and timber glowing like a pillar of fire. At 6.30pm the crowd detected signs of collapse, and gradually swaying, the structure heeled over in a northern direction, and fell into the churchyard, and nothing was left on the roof but half a dozen timbers, which slowly fell inside the walls.

By 7.30pm the fire had exhausted itself in the body of the church, and the chancel, was announced to be saved, the fireman having got the upper hand of the flames. The top of the square tower was still on fire, and without pressure of water nothing could be done there.

Among the clergy on the scene were the Rev.G.A.Hale (who has charge of the parish in his father's illness), the Rev.W.M.Bottome (Vicar of "All Saints", Galley Hill), and the Rev.M.M.Ffinch (Chaplain of "Huggens" College Northfleet). The Rev.G.A.Hale who seemed in much distress, was seen to mount a ladder and enter the chancel windows several times as the fire raged within.

Eyewitness, Mrs Hazell. Of the "Blue Anchor." High Street, only a few yards from the church, saw the building struck. She was standing at the door watching the storm overhead, when, as she put it, "A fearful flash came right across the street, and seemed to go right into the church, and in a minute or two I saw fire in the lower windows of the church. The peal of the thunder which followed seemed to shake the whole place. It seemed as if n awful ball of fire rushed right down the street." Many other residents spoke of the awfulness of the appearance of the great flash and the terror caused by the peal of thunder which followed.

There is a feeling of profound sympathy with the Rector Rev.G.Hale, at the time away on holiday at Cornwall. Following so close upon his terrible loss of his son in the Boar War in South Africa, this second blow is particularly terrible. To the parishioners generally it is a loss of deep regret that they have lost a priceless legacy and much loved church.

Drawing of the church after the fire (by C T Youens

25

The Restoration of Swanscombe Church

The Gravesend Standard Sept 1902

The restoration of the parish church of Swanscombe by Mr Jabez Bignall, who restored the church 28 years ago (1874), is about to commence, and is expected to occupy about six months. It restoring the screen, the architect will be assisted by a carefully measured drawing executed by Mr Frank J Walker, and which appeared in the builders journal last week. The amount received from insurance will probably be £2,065. The last restoration by Mr George White, cost from £3,000 to £4,000.

A public meeting was held on Wednesday evening last week at Church House, Galley Hill, lent by the Rev W M Bottome to elect a restoration committee and receive the architect's report. About 30 attended, including the Rector the Rev G Hale, the Rev G A Hale's curate, the Rev M M Ffinch, the Rev C T Whitmell, Mr J Carter churchwarden, the sidesmen, and several bell ringers.

The Rector read a letter from the Rev W M Bottome, saying he would attend if possible, but if prevented would be glad to be elected a member of the committee, and would do all in his power to aid their efforts.

The Rector, in his absence of the Rev W M Bottome, who was to have presided, was voted to the Chair, and the Rev G A Hale was asked to act as secretary for the meeting.

The Chairman explained the object of the meeting, and stated that the church had been insured for £2,550, of which, they expected to get £2,065. It would be necessary to raise about £1,900 besides, in order to restore the church to the state in which it was before the fire, the cost of which in the architect's opinion would be about £4,000. He added that it was their important duty to avoid vandalism in the restoration of so ancient a building.

The Rev M M Ffinch (Northfleet) proposed the formation of a restoration committee, remarking that he had and loved the old church for nearly 40 years, and well remembered preaching there in the year 1870.

The Rev C T Whitmell seconded the resolution, and expressed deep sympathy with the work, and readiness to serve on the committee as Rector of the eldest daughter Church St Botolph Northfleet

The Chairman said he had written to Mr F A White and requested him, in view of the deep interest he had taken in the welfare of Swanscombe, to serve on the committee, and to allow him to propose him as chairman. As however he was abroad, he had not yet received a reply. He had also written to Mr J Bazley White, Mr Leedham White, Mr Thomas Bevan (who has served on the restoration committee 28 year previous (1874) , and Alderman John Russell, asking leave to place their names on the committee. He had received a *telegram* from Alderman Russell:----"Sorry I cannot attend meeting. "stop" Shall be pleased to help restoration "stop",---- JOHN RUSSELL,". He proposed that the committee should consist of the Rector, the Rev G A Hale, and the churchwardens and sidesmen *ex-officio*, and also the following gentlemen, subject to their consent:---*The Rev W M Bottome (Vicar of "All Saints" Galley Hill), the Rev C T Whitmell Rector of "Greenhite", the Rev M M Ffinch (Chaplain of "Huggens" College) the Rev H Bingham Stevens "Darenth", and Rev.Canon F W Murray "Rector of Stone", Commander G O Moore, Commander T Triggs, Commander Smith, Dr Gwya Jones, Messers, F A White, J Bazley White, Leedham White, Thomas Bevan, T C Coyler-Fergusson, J Hoyle, F Watt, R C Styles, J Cubitt, John Russell, Charles Hewitt, Walter Ames, and W Harper.*

Mr Walter Ames seconded the resolution, which was carried unanimously. The Chairman then read the following communication from the architect.

"Wimbledon, August 17th 1902"

"In accordance with your request, I visited SS Peter and Paul Church, Swanscombe yesterday. The chief work to be done is mostly confined to the new woodwork, new nave roof, north and south aisle, new wood spire and floor to tower. Also the re-seating of nave and aisle repairs to the stonework, and fabric generally. The loss of the bells the ancient screen and the almost total destruction of the font and stained glass windows, are the losses most missed. I could not yesterday, without a proper ladders and scaffolding examine thoroughly the tower walls, but I fear much upon proper examination, they will require to be carefully taken down and rebuilt before we can in a new floor, and put on the weight of a new spire and the new bells. To restore the building to its original appearance, including new bells, stained glass, etc will cost about £4,000. I will push on the drawing and specification, so that we may commence the work early in September 1902. I have written to four builders to know if they will be willing to send tenders for the work.

"Faithfully Yours'

"J Bignell, Architect"

First postcard of the newly restored church 1903, and below 2011

The Restoration Concert Programme 18th February 1903

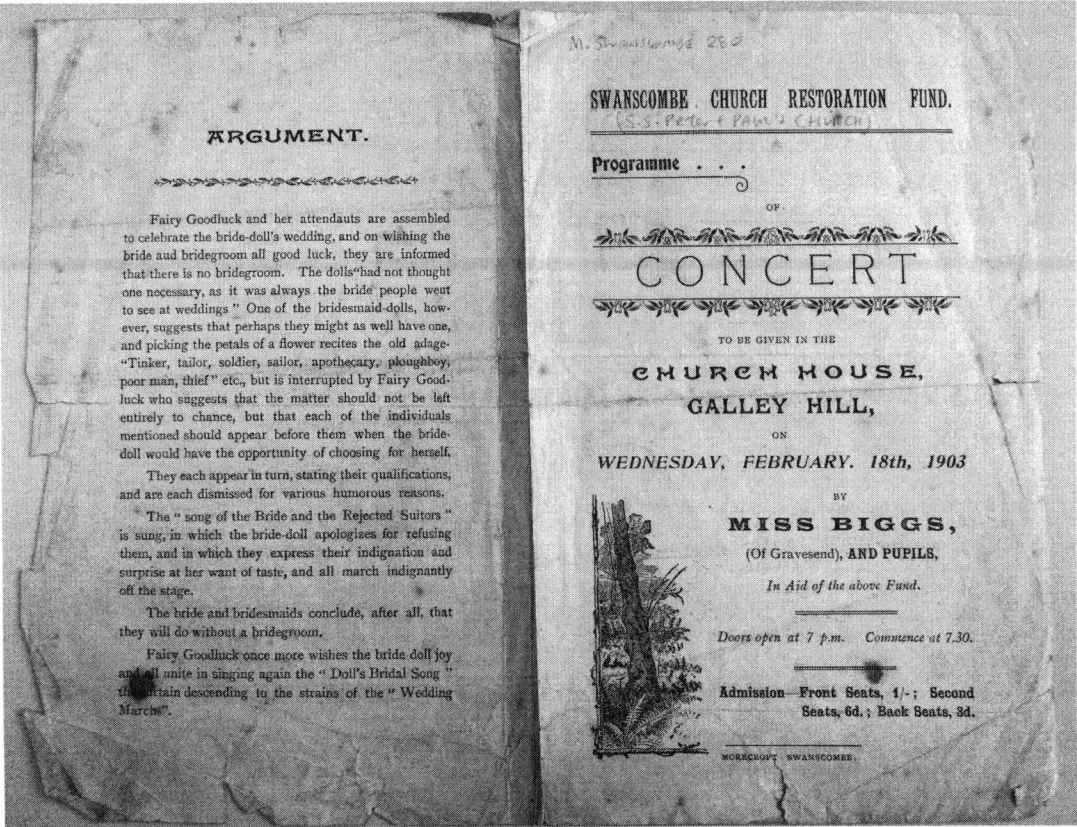

A List of donations from the inhabitants of Swanscombe

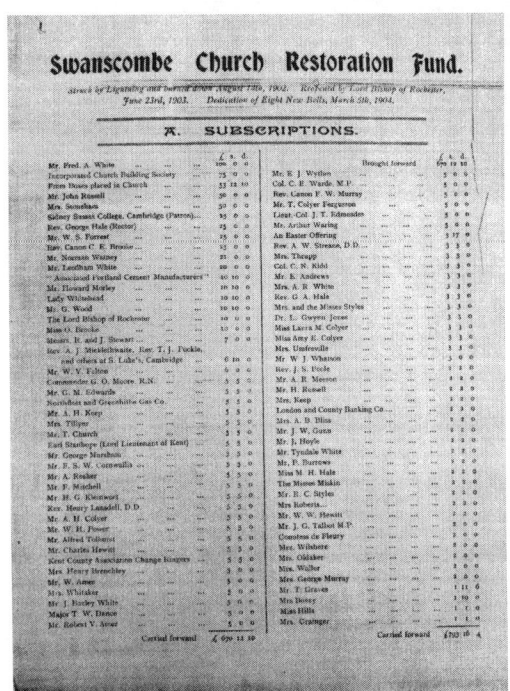

The Exterior

As we survey it today, Swanscombe church shows work of many periods, Saxon, Norman, Early English and later craftsmen have left their mark upon the fabric. The building consists of nave and aisles chancel, tower and north porch, Restoration in 1873-4 and again after the fire 1902 have given the church fabric a more youthful appearance than its age would seen to suggest.

The Lower part of the tower is Saxon or very early Norman. Certainly the south facing window in this lower part of the tower is Saxon, it is double splayed and is built with Roman tiles bricks. (The Romans had a settlement at Springhead to the south east of Swanscombe on the Dover Road). The tower itself, sturdy and solid, is of stone and rubble with a two light west window of the Decorated Period and several small lancets to the bell chamber. The tower is capped by a short stumpy broach steeple of shingles. It forms in fact, a typical 'Home Counties" spire.

Exterior Churchyard 1930

External View 2011

The Interior

We enter the church through the North Porch which, as before mentioned, was rebuilt in 1874 in memory of Erasmus Wilson FRS, of Stone, the porch is quite spacious with double columns at the entrance.

The NAVE dates from the 13th century and is the Early English style of architecture. The North and South arcades are each of 3-pointed arches with round columns, each having a different capital motive, The Nave roof is of open beamwork. Above the arcading are the windows of the former clerestory. These have been blocked up by the timberwork of the aisle roofs which were, at some period, raised to meet the nave roof level.

At the west end a screen fills the tower opening. (The original arch from the nave has now gone). It was made by MR F J Ring of this parish and is in the style of the screen removed from the chancel arch, which dated from 1250 and which was destroyed by the fire in 1902. The screen, which is quite plain in style was placed here in 1935.

Alongside the screen is an ancient chalk font which is said to be of the Norman period. However, as at that time fonts were usually made of French stone, this Swanscombe font may be Saxon in origin. Cut from a solid block of chalk it has carved upon it the emblems of the four evangelists. It was badly damaged in post reformation times and again in 1902 fire when it was broken into pieces, it had been fitted into a wooden casing which was completely burnt. The older part of the font, the chalk basin stands on one large and four small marble columns, which terminate in a stone base slab.

The lower part of the tower walls are of Saxon masonry (or, at latest, early Norman) and Saxon, too, is the double light window with its Roman tile brickwork. It may be seen high on the south wall of the tower. Double splayed windows such as this (that is, with the narrowest part in the very centre of the wall) are rare indeed and almost always indicate Saxon craftsmanship.

The western window of the tower is a Decorated one of two lights and with quite simple tracery. It shows Saint Peter in one light and Saint Paul in the other. Saint Peter holding a bunch of keys. The window, which has the most beautiful colours, is in memory of those Swanscombe service personnel and civilians who died in the 1939-45 war. Designed by F D Farrar Bell, it replaces the former patronal window, destroyed by blast in the last war. It was dedicated in September, 1960, by the Archdeacon of Rochester.

The tower has a peal of eight bells. On one wall nearby is a wooden memorial tablet to W H Harper who was churchwarden, bell-ringer and chairman until his death in 1928

At the nave's east end is a very rare feature, an ancient wooden lectern. Few of those now survive in our parish churches. This one is of the 15th century and has a double desk allowing for a book on either side. Attached to its fluted wooden pillar are two iron staples to which were fastened the chains that once held the Bible, in days when books were so precious that they had to be so guarded.

On the opposite of the chancel arch is the Jacobean pulpit, of quite plain wooden paneling with only the panel edges carved.

In the nave floor are two ancient grave slabs. One is in memory of John Bayly whom died in 1791, , aged 65 (and also to his wife), whilst the other is a slab with brasses to the memory of William Tuckey who died in 1800, Aged 84. Only two tablets adorn the walls of the nave, one of these is to Lucy Styles who died in 1906, It was placed here by members of the Mothers' Meeting and Girls' Friendly Society.

South Aisle,
we find much of interest, In the outer wall is a leper window, blocked on the outside, whilst in the same wall are the stairs that once led to the rood loft, a now vanished feature.

Also on the south outer wall is a rather beautiful roll of honour that tells the names of the fallen of the Two Great Wars 1914-18 – 1938-45, and a shelf for wreaths and flowers.

At the west end is a small lancet window with a Latin inscribed brass beneath and a pattern of colour in its panels. At the east end behind the altar is a painting of the Virgin and Child, a copy painted by a daughter of a former rector, and a handsome two light window showing, in rich colours, the figures of St Martin and St Cecilia.

Alongside the altar is a mediaeval piscine and an elaborate wall memorial tablet to Anthony Weldon. He was the son of Sir Ralph Weldon and died in 1613 at the age of 65. Set in an elaborate framing of shields and scrolls he is shown dressed in Elizabethan attire kneeling at a reading desk.

On the south wall are two windows of clear glass and on with stained glass. It illustrates the theme "Jesus said unto them come ye after me" and "Beginning to sink, he cried, saying, Lord save me." Also on this wall is a picture from the Bible, in memory of Isabel Abraham, who died in 1912.. By the altar is a tattered and worn flag from London's Cenotaph. It was given to Greenhithe Old Contemptibles and in 1935 placed here in Swanscombe church, the mother church of both Swanscombe and Greenhithe.

There are a number of grave slabs in the south aisle floor at the eastern end. Most are of the 18th century, one of the most interesting being to Ann, the Relict of Percivall Hart, Knight, of Lullingstone Castle. She died in May 1712, Another is to Elinor, the Relict of William Say. She died in 1678. Among the wall tablets to 19th century worshippers is one to Lieutenant Thomas Sharp Hill, Royal Navy, who was killed whilst serving on H.M.S. "Inconstant" at Smyrna in Turkey.

In this aisle, too, is the church's most elaborate treasure, the great Weldon tomb and monument. It is to Sir Ralph Weldon and Lady Elizabeth Weldon who lived in the 16th – 17th Centuries. Sir Ralph was the chief Clerk Controller to King James I. He died aged 64 in 1609, He is shown in armour reclining on his side as if in conversation with his wife who lies on her back in full Elizabethan gown and ruffs. Behind them are the family arms and crests and below them a frieze of their three sons and five of their six daughters (Katherine, Anne, Elizabeth Mary, Lydeth and Barbara). The children are kneelng are also dressed in period costume. On either side of them are patterns of entwined bones, spades, scythes and vines whilst this motto is also seen.

> "Let this suffice for those who hereby pass
> to signify how, when and what he was,
> And for his life, his change and honest fame
> He hath well done, and so made good his name,"

In 1955 the monument, which is adorned with scrolls and flourishes, was cleaned and restored by the Hon. Mrs Dickinson of Aylesbury, with the help of ladies of Swanscombe parish.

North Aisle

we find structurally a similar part of the building, 13th century aisle of short proportions. Of the four windows only one is coloured glass. It is the east window and shows the Resurrection of Christ. As a nearby brass tells this window, was put in by a committee to commemorate the church's first restoration in 1873 by Professor, Erasmus Wilson FRS. This eastern end of the north aisle forms a Wilson Chapel for here are several 19th century tablets to members of the family a well as the flamboyant marble tomb of Sir Erasmus Wilson himself. The tomb is adorned with family crests and coats of arms. As a tablet tells us Sir Erasmus Wilson was born in 1809 an died in 1884. He rose to be the President of the Royal College of Surgeons and was also a leading Freemason and responsible for a multitude of public works (not least being the 1873-4 restoration of Swanscombe Church).

Chancel

we see late Saxon or Norman work in the outer walls, though the sanctuary is of a later date. In the floor are a number of 18th century grave slabs of some interest. One is to Thomas Knights a merchant of London who died in 1676 another is to John Taylor, a rector here who died in 1757.

The Choir

stalls are of plain design and the altar rails of attractive twisted balusters. The altar itself is backed by curtains and has the Mothers' Union banner as guardian. By the altar is a piscina of the late mediaeval period.

On the north wall is the organ (built by Henry Fincham of London) and a number of 19th century tablets and memorials of largely local interest. This wall is pierced by a single long narrow lancet filled with patterned glass in memory of Charles Brandt who died in 1876, aged fifty. He was on of the founders of the Erasmus Wilson Lodge of Freemasons. Here too, we see a painting of Christ after His decent from the Cross.

The east window is the largest in the church and one of the most beautiful. Its three lights show Jesus surrounded by His apostles and with, in the lower portions, the Lamb of God and other symbols. The entire window is rich in colour and illustrates the theme "Jesus Christ the same yesterday, today and for ever". The window is "To the Glory of God and in memory of the men of this church and parish who gave their lives in the 1914-18 war".

On the south side of the Sanctuary there is a two light window of clear glass and in the chancel two light stained glass window depicting the theme, "Let me find grace in thy sight". The Lord recompense thee thy work", form the story of Boaz and Ruth, from the book of Ruth. Showing two saints in subdued colours, this lovely window is in memory of the parents of William and Mary Russell, being inserted by them in 1904.

Also in the chancel are the two 19th century memorial tablets. The most interesting is the Dame Elinor Weldon, who died aged 86, in 1622. She is shown in her Elizabethan robes and ruff kneeling in prayer with the scrolls and flamboyance of the period.

These, then are the treasures of Swanscombe Church. For over a thousand years a church has stood on this site and these very walls incorporate stones that are nine centuries old or more. In contrast to the stark simplicity of these early builders' work we see also the flamboyance of mediaeval tombs and memorials. The contrast between richness and simplicity is embodied in the very essence of the church and is at once its finest feature.

Outside view of the Church c1935

Internal View's 1930

The Invicta Monument

This monument depicts the meeting of Men of Kent and Kentish Men with the Invader William Duke of Normandy after the battle of Hastings

East End of the Church 2011

Swanscombe Rectory

Swanscombe Rectory c1915

Swanscombe Rectory. This wonderful building was another victim of a trend within the Church of England to sell off assets and replace them with smaller modern houses and this happened at Swanscambe in the early 1960s. This building was constructed, by Reverend George Cecil Renouard (Rector 1818-1867), who ran a private school from its extensive rooms. One of the pupils was Sir Erasmus Wilson (1809-1884), who became a great surgeon, brought Cleopatra's needle to London and gave much money for the church's restoration in 1873. Renouard's rectory replaced an earlier structure, which doubled as a rectory and farm – the latter bringing in an income for the rector. A successor to Renouard as rector was Reverend Thomas Candy (rector 1868-1888) who established an early public library in a room in this building from 1887. The present rectory and church centre stand on the site of this building as well as some housing development. (From Christoph Bull "Swanscombe in old picture postcards" 2005)

Swanscombe Church, Oast Houses, Rectory c1910

List of Rectors

1320	John Lett	1567	Thomas Withers
	John Calabar	1569	Peter Henley
	William Cres	1576	Thomas Carter
1332	Edmund de London	1596	Tertullian Pine
1349	John Melbourne	1606	Richard Betts
	John Denet de Burton	1620	James Iken
1360	Robert de Crull	1641	Richard Betts
	Robert Strutt	1655	William Hopkins
1363	Richard Rail	1665	John Watts
1369	Ralphe Bolewhye	1670	William Hopkins
	John ate Vyne	1686	John Hope
1389	Richard Cotynsham	1705	Henry Bosse
1390	John Skeftalyng	1737	John Taylor
1391	Thomas Ruggelye	1757	Martin Barnes
1392	John de Stoke	1760	John Lawson
1393	John Forster	1781	Edward Oliver
1397	John Wynter	1818	George C Renouard
1413	Richard Shelley	1867	James Yates
1426	Thomas Banester	1868	Thomas H Candy
1432	Thomas Pikene	1889	George Hale
1442	James Hamelyn	1917	Edward F C Ward
1446	Robert Blakstow	1940	John Henry Weller
1452	William Collett	1956	Robert D Sawyer
1462	Reginald Thomas	1969	Robert David Silk
1493	Peter Greaves	1976	John R Hambidge
1514	William Ingalnde	1985	Timothy J Mercer
1516	John Knight	1996	David Scott
1526	Gilbert Lathan	2012	Mark Hurley (Priest in charge)
1546	William Saxey		

NOOKS AND CORNERS OF OLD ENGLAND

Article in the local paper 26th November 1842

Swanscombe is one of many picturesque villages, which so pleasantly margin "Old Father Thames" as he flows steadily on between Kent and Essex to the sea. The fatal Niger, the mighty Amazon, the picturesque and historic Rhine, the classic Tiber, each and all have their scenes, their stories and associations. Each by turn claims notice, and each has goodly claim to attention. But commend us, and all Englishmen to the Thames.

SWANSCOMBE CHURCH.

Swanscombe, whose church is here chosen for illustration, being well surrounded by wood, has a highly picturesque appearance from the Thames, which forms the northern boundary of the parish. It is near Northfleet, and about four miles from Dartford, and no great distance from Gravesend and Greenhite, a spot familiar to the river tourist, being one of its hamlets. A Kentish Village, with now about a thousand inhabitants, it has its share of Kentish History.

Swanscombe Church is the subject of our above sketch. It is chiefly in the early English Style, and is dedicated to St Peter, and in old times, was much "frequented by pilgrims, who resorted hither for St Hilderfirth's help." This saint was a bishop, and had a shrine there, with his portrait in the upper window of the south side. He was supposed to have the power to cure insanity. The church contains a number tombs to the memory of the later possessors of the manor, and of other inhabitants of the parish, as one always wishes, and almost expects, so to see in an ancient village church.

SWANSCOMBE: Church reopens after renovations

By Michael Purton »

A CHURCH has reopened after a renovation which saw 43 bodies discovered in unmarked graves.

On January 11 around 160 people attended St Peter and St Paul's Church in Swanscombe Street, Swanscombe, to celebrate its reopening after a £275,000 transformation.

Renovations, which included repairing the church tower and installing central heating, were funded by the Colyer-Fergusson Charitable Trust, which provides grants to churches and charities across Kent.

Rev David Scott invited News Shopper to look around the refurbished church.

The 68-year-old said: "The work had been needed for a long time and we are all very excited to get into the new church.

"The central heating is obviously very welcome, especially with the current cold weather.

"I know the congregation will be very pleased not to be freezing during services."

From the beginning of the renovation in August through to late October, 43 bodies were found in unmarked graves while the church cemetery was dug-up for drainage work.

Archaeologist Guy Seddon, who oversaw the work in the graveyard, said: "The bodies found included men, women and children and the majority of them seem to be around 200 to 300 years old."

Mr Seddon, who has been an archaeologist for 14 years and works for London-based Pro Construct Archaeology, says the graves were probably unmarked because the tombstones had been displaced over the years.

The bodies were held in storage until work on the cemetery was finished in early November and were then buried again, with Rev Scott performing a service.

The current church building was first put up around the 12th century, although stones in the south wall of the tower were first laid around 1050.

It is the oldest building in Swanscombe.

Article in the Newshopper 27th January 2009

Some Monumental Inscriptions of **Swanscombe** Church,

Noted by Leland L. Duncan 4 June 1922.
Typed up by Ted Connell, checked by Frank & Zena Bamping

Square monument in railings: Mrs Susanna HURST wife of James Hurst died 23 May 1789 aged 26 years. Also 2 children of above died in infancy.

Mr Silas CHAPMAN died 21 June 1819 aged 40 years. Kitty Chapman his wife died 20 June 1844 aged 70 years.

2. Mr Francis ELAND late of this Parish died 8 October 1775 aged 75 years.

3. Mr William WARE of this Parish died 11 February 1834 in his 76th years. Mrs Elizabeth Ware his wife died 4 July 1841 aged 78 years. Sarah daughter of above and wife of Mr BLISS of this Parish died 10th April 1838 aged 40 years. Emily Ann wife of Mr A. B. Bliss of this Parish died 23 March 1865 aged 36 years.

4. Mr Rowland WARE born in this Parish 30 October 1761 died 11 May 1846. These stones are raised by the remaining children of Rowland and Ann Ware.

5. Mrs Ann WARE wife of Mr Rowland Ware died 21 June 1821 aged 57 years. Also Rowland Ware son of above died 26 May 1818 aged 19 years.

6, Mr Jonathan WARE late of this Parish, yeoman died 27 February 1797 aged 77 years. Mr Ann Ware late wife of above died 11 November 1779 aged 66 years.

7. Mrs Sarah RIXSON 2nd wife of George Rixson of this Parish died 30 July 1789 aged 44 years.

8. Mr William SMALL yeoman of this Parish died 22 August 1758 aged 31 years. Sarah daughter of the above William and Elizabeth Small lies buried in a lead coffin in the grave she died 2 June 1765 aged 9 years.

9. Mr George POWSEY died 21(?) November 1801 aged 30 years. Verse.

10. Mr John POWSEY of the Parish of Northfleet died 23 February 1794 aged 63 years. Elizabeth his wife died 5 May 1802 aged 67 years.

11. Philip POWSEY son of John and Elizabeth Powsey of Northfleet died 19 January 1786 aged 19 years.

12. Mr James POWSEY of the Parish of Northfleet died 25 April 1803 aged 34 years.

13. Ann RIXSON wife of George Rixson and daughter of Thomas POWSEY of this Parish died 23 September 1773 aged 27 years.

14. Thomas POWSEY for many years Clerk of this Parish died 10 June 1779 aged 61 years. Elizabeth Powsey wife of above died 19 March 1783 aged 70 years. .

15. Mary wife of Henry MARTIN of this Parish daughter of George HARDS of Dartford died 1 November 1766 aged (?50) years. .

15a. Lefthand side: Sarah MARTIN aged 5 years died 1759. Righthand side: Margaret Martin aged 1 year died 1758.

16. Mrs Ann LAVENDER wife of Mr John Lavender died 20 May 17(?93) aged 75 years. *[Register: 1793 May 23 Anne LAVENDER, widow buried F+ZB]*

17. Headstone broken: Mary Ann WALLIS of this Parish died 8 December 1844 aged 32 years. Also (?William) Wallis husband of above died 31 December 1888 aged 83 years.

18. Elizabeth WILLIAMS died 13 September 1842 aged 42 years. Also Page 8Keziah WATTS her sister died 24 September 1846 aged 40 years.

19. Edwin CHALLIS died 16 December 1843 aged 4 years. .

20. Mr John BARTLETT, mason died 6 December 1833 aged 24 years. North East corner of graveyard

21. Footstone: M.A.W. 1844 W.W. 1887

22. Charles Robert CURTIS died 16 December 1835 aged 25 years. Henry Curtis died 14 February 1836 aged 24 years.

23. Ann wife of William MUNN of this Parish died 14 May 1862 aged 63 years. Above William Munn died 4 October 1883 aged 79 years.

24. Sophia wife of John MUNN of the Parish of Longfield died 20 November 1853 aged 72 years. Above John Munn died 5 May 1863 aged 83 years.

25. Mrs Mary Ann TOLHURST died 24 December 1825 aged 29 years. Thomas Tolhurst died 4 December 1823 aged 3 weeks. Mr Thomas Tolhurst of this Parish died 28 July 1849 aged 49 years. Charles Edmeades son of the above Mr Thomas Tolhurst and Jane Elizabeth his 2nd wife died 18 December 1850 aged 18 years. Jane Elizabeth wife of the above Mr Thomas Tolhurst died 2 December 1884 in her 85th year. Thomas Edmeades Tolhurst son of Thomas and Jane Tolhurst died at Northfleet 21 June 188(?5) aged 57 years.

26. In memory of William McBEATH late late M _ _ ross in the Royal Artillery who died 5 June 1775 aged 32 years. Who in his military character was respected by his Officers Beloved by his equals and much lamented by his friends ' 8 lines of verse'

27. Mr Benjamin ARLETT of this Parish died 29 April 1829 aged 83 years.

28. Mr George ARLETT of Greenhithe in this Parish died 18 January 1842 aged 64 years. Sarah his wife died 4 May 1842 aged 65 years.

29.William Henry ARLETT of this Parish died 14 December 1848 aged 40 years.

30. Coffin shaped slab: Elizabeth wife of George Thomas SWETTENHAM died 31 May 1832 aged 41 years. Ann Swettenham daughter of above died February 1824 aged 3 weeks.

31. Ann wife of John PRIME of this Parish died 11 December 1855 aged 65 years. John Prime died 21 January 1864 aged 58 years.

32. Here lies the body of Henry EDWARDS of Rye in Sussex who died of smallpox at this place on board the vessel of which he was Page 13Master the 25 April 1763 aged 51 years. He left issue a disconsolate widow, 2 daughters and 1 son. His character both in publick and private capacity was such as to leave not an enemy behind and who himself endeavoured to be the friend of everyone.

33. Henry William son of Mr George ANDREWS and Charlotte his wife of Greenhithe died 18 April 1848 in his 18th year. Elizabeth Ann died 1 January 1844 aged 7 months. Above Mr George Andrews died 17 July 1849 aged 53 years. He left issue by Charlotte his wife 4 sons and 4 daughters.

34. Flat stone: Mrs Elizabeth HARE wife of Mr John Hare died 22 October 1775 aged 70 years.Also the above Mr John Hare died 8 April 1787 aged 87 years.

35. Mr William HENDEN late of this Parish died 27 January 1802 aged 68 years. Mrs Sarah PHILLIPS wife of Mr James LAWRANCE Phillips and daughter of above died 27 February 1803 aged 21 years.

36. (Decayed) Mr John WOODWARD died May _ _ 1847 aged _ _ Footstone J. W. 1847, C. W. 1861

37. Mr Thomas SHEPHERD son of John and Ann Shepherd of this Parish died 20 December 1815 aged 18 years. A sudden death, a mind contented he lived beloved and died lamented. Edward Shepherd died 27 May 1819 aged 13 years. George Shepherd died 18 February 1821 aged 13 years. Also Thomas, William and James died in infancy. Walter Shepherd died 10 October 1832 in 30th years. John Shepherd father of above died 10 November 1833 aged 72 years. Footstones: E.S. 1819, G.S. 1821, W.S. 1832, G.S. 1821, E.S. 1810, T.S. 1815, J.S. 1833.

38. Mr Sampson WATERS of this Parish died 8 June 1846 aged 71 years.

39. Mrs Elizabeth MORRIS wife of Cartwright Morris Esq. of Greenhithe died 22 June 1795 aged (?5)6 years. Charles MORRIS son of above obit died 5 July 1791 aged 19 years.

40. Charles WILKS Esq formerly of Purfleet Essex and late of Greenhithe died 17 November 1847 aged 87 years, 64 of which he served in Her Majesty's Navy and Ordnance.

41. Elizabeth HALL wife of Ambrose Hall of this Parish died 5 June 1779 aged 70 years. The above Ambrose Hall died 8 December 1793 aged 93 years.

42. Frederick William infant son of Frederick and Lucy ABBOTT of Pustwell House in this Parish died 10 April 1861 aged 10 months. *[PUSTWELL family appear in the registers in the 1550's F+Z B]*

43. Raymond Reginald infant son of James and Mary Elizabeth VOGAN of Greenhithe died 26 September 1858 aged 8 months. Harry James likewise son of above died 6 February 1859 aged 4 years 4 months. Also their sister, Mary died 15 August 1862 aged 5 weeks. Frederick Overall Vogan son of above died 9 May 1865 in his 10th year.

44. Richard Edward WEST Esq. late of the Borough of Southwark and of this Parish died 6 October 1857 aged 68 years.

45. Mr John SMALL of this Parish died 28 September 1825 aged 73 years. William Small son of the above died 22 August 1826 aged 12 years and 8 months. Mrs Ann Small wife of the above Mr John Small died 28 September 1832 aged 49 years. Mr John Small son of above John and Ann Small died 13 March 1842 aged 30 (or 32) years.

46. Tankerville Drew INGALL born 19 April 1857, died 23 July 1858. Helen Maria Ingall born 2 January 1860 died 28 February 1862. Cedric Drew Ingall born 7 July 1867, died 9 July 1867. Jane DREW grandmother of above died 13 October 1881 aged 80 years.

47.. Selina the much loved granddaughter of Mrs Mary Ann WHITEHEAD of Greenhithe died 18 August 1847 aged 7 years.

48. Cross head stone: Laura Mitford BRAMWELL died 13 July 1859 aged 11 years.

49. Cross head stone: Charles William BY Esq. died 16 October 1864 aged 83 years. Charlotte his wife died 30 October 1864 aged 82 years.

50. Catherine wife of William COSSART Esq of St Johns Wood London died at Greenhithe 12 October 1845 aged 26 years.

51. William Stephen HOADLEY husband of Ann Hoadley died 27 January 1863 aged 55 years. The above Ann Hoadley of Greenhithe died aged years. [not filled in on headstone]

52. Mr Robert DONNE Senior died 2 December 1836 aged 73 years

53. Elizabeth DONNE late wife of Charles Doone of the Parish of St Saviours Southwark died 5 November 1847 aged 60 years. An affectionate mother and wife. Above Charle Donne 30 January 1873 aged 76 years.

54. Hannah DONNE died 30 October 1848 aged 49 years. James Doone died 16 January 1865 aged 66 years.

55. Mary CHAPMAN daughter of Edward and Mary Chapman of Greenhithe in this Parish died 21 March 1801 in her 24th year.

56. Low flat tomb: Mr John WOOTTON late of this Parish died 22 January 1764 aged 56. Also Mary his wife died 5 March 1778 aged 71 years. Also Mr Richard Wootton of Northfleet, native of Greenhithe in this Parish died 10 August 1796 aged 59 years. Also Mrs Mary Wootton of Northfleet wife of the above Mr Richard Wootton died 18 October 1828 in his 86th year.

57. Large brick altar tomb with stone top: Mary wife of John HILL of the Parish Swanscombe died 6 November 1740 aged 42 years.

58. Richard WHISKIN of Greenhithe died 15 June 1796 aged 38 years. James Whiskin son of above died 26 June 1830 aged 37 years. Mary Whiskin relict of above died 12 May 1834 aged 84 years.

59. Thomas HEWITT died 21 January 1857 aged 44 years. Elizabeth daughter of above died 17 May 1849 aged 7 years. North of Tower:

60. Robert RICHARDSON Esq late of Honourable East India Company Bengal Civil Service died 17 June 1847 aged 66 years.

61. Eliza wife of Mr Peter VITOU of Greenhithe in this Parish died 15 November 1854 aged 61 years. Above Mr Peter Vitou died 15

January 1858 aged 75 years. Elizabeth daughter of above died 20 January 1871 aged 53 years. Louisa PARSONS eldest daughter of above and relict of Joseph Parsons (late of Barkingside Essex) died 21 October 1880 aged 67 years. Also Sarah Vitou daughter of above died 19 December 1895 aged 73 years. .

62. Altar tomb: Top Here lyeth the body of Ma _ _ _ _ KINGSLAND late? Wife of Mr John Kingsland of this Parish who departed January 17[?5] aged 54(?9) years. She lived . . . . .mother . . . . Here lyeth the body of Mr John EVEREST of this Parish who departed this life _ _ May 1732 aged 67 years. 3 lines of verse North side: In this vault beneath whose silence had not previously been invaded for nearly a century are interred the remains of Judith Sarah STEVENS the wife of Mr William Stevens solicitor of Hatton Garden. The only grandchild and heir at law of William EVEREST Esq formerly of Fawkham in this County by his daughter Mildred who married Mr William Stevens of Woodmanstone in Surrey. The above named Judith Sarah was the th _ _ _ daughter of the late Mr Samuel KING formerly of Yarmouth and afterwards of Beccles in Suffolk. She died on the 17th day of January 1832 aged 61 years. Her father and mother whose maiden name was JAY were both eminently pious christians and brought up their children in the fear of God and their daughter Judith Sarah followed their bright example in fulfilling the various duties of the daughter, the sister, the wife, the mother and the friend. She was uniformly exemplary taking the Holy Scripture as the only rule of her faith and conduct. Her husband and children with an _ _ _ (4 more lines.

63. Henry HOLLAND died 19 November 1719 aged 37 years.

64. Cross opposite tower: William GOSTLING died 31 Julu 1890 aged 58 years. Elizabeth his wife died 3 February 1893 aged 57 years.

65. Mr John SMALL yeoman of this Parish died 19th December 1757 aged 63 years. He left issue by his first wife Sarah one son William Small who survived his father 3 months and 3 days,

66. Margaret SMALL widow of John Small died 10th February 1763 aged 79 years.

67. Altar tomb: Top: Mr Harry MASON late of Cross Lane London died 26 September 1802 aged 26 years. Also Edward Harden Mason died 5 October 1819 aged 57 years. North side Mr Edward Mason of this Parish died (?17) July 1768 aged 6(?7) years. South side Mr Henry Mason of this Parish died 21 May 1781 aged __ years. Also Mr Harry Mason died 26 September 1802 aged 26 years.

68. Large tomb in railings. North side: The family vault of William COLYER of this Parish died 12 October 1846 aged 93 years. Christian his wife died 21 August 1804 aged 52 years. West end: Ann wife of Thomas Page 34Colyer died 28 October 1854 aged 62 years. Thomas Colyer above named died 12 May 1860 aged 69 years. South side: Eliza daughter of Thomas Colyer died 19 April 1836. Elizabeth wife of William Colyer died 20 July 1850 aged 35 years. William Colyer above named died 12 September 1856 aged 39 years.

69. Mrs Sarah FULLJAMES wife of Mr Edward Fulljames of this Parish died 5 July 1770 aged 48 years. Also Mr Edward Fulljames died 4 August 1781 aged 66 years. Also Edward Fulljames son of the above died 26 February 1800 aged 48 years.

70. *Mr Robert DURLING of the Parish of Stone died 14 September 1833 in his 77th year.*

71. Mrs Elizabeth DAVIDSON relict of the late Mr Robert Timothy Davidson of the City of Rochester and daughter of Robert and Ann Durling of the Parish of Stone died 28 December 1829 in her 36th year. Also Mary Durling of Stone Wood 4th and last surviving daughter of the above Robert and Ann Durling died 13 August 1854 aged 57 years.

72. *Mrs Ann DURLING wife of Mr Robert Durling of the Parish of Stone died 9 November 1827 in her 73rd year.*

73. Mrs Sarah WARNER wife of Mr James Warner of this Parish died 13 January 1815 aged 49 years. Mr James Warner died 15 April 1832 aged 79 years.

74. Ann GRAY wife of Caleb Gray died 6 March 1812 aged 30 years. Mr Caleb Gray husband of above died 6 July 1825 aged 56 years. Also Elizabeth FIELDER died 15 April 1827 aged 71 years.

75. Mrs Ann SIMMONS wife of Mr Thomas Simmons died 19 July 1809 aged 19 years. Also Ann Simmons daughter of above died 18 February 1810 aged 6 months. Mrs Elizabeth HORLOCK died 24 April 1856 aged 72 years. Mr Samuel Horlock died 18 December 1863 aged 82 years. Alice Martin Horlock died 16 June 1865 aged ?11 years.

76. Mr John HAYES late of Pitsey in Essex died 30 November 1795 aged 59 years. Mrs Rebecca Hayes wife of above died 5 April 1818 aged 84 years.

77. Mr William Bray MUSGROVE late of the pr _ _ _ _ _ _ Yarmouth died September 185(?4) aged 41 years. Also Maria Louisa Musgrove died 30 September 1872 aged 58 years.

78. John FELDWICK of Greenhithe died 5 June 1839 aged 79 years. Also Joanna wife of above died 9 December 1847 aged 80 years.

79. Mr Edmund FARMER-FRANCIS died 23 September 1833 aged 26 years. Also Edmund Farmer-Francis son of above died 17 March 1833 aged 3 months and 3 days.

80. John PIRKINS of the Parish of Stone died 28 February 1742 aged 71 years.

81. Elizabeth HOLDAWAY daughter of Edward and Mary Ann Holdaway died _ February 1811 aged _ _ (gone). Also Mary Ann Holdaway wife of Edward Holdaway died 15 March 1811 aged [?3]2 or [?72] years of age.

82. Lieutenant George SOWTON late of His Majesty's Ship JUNO died 8 February 1803 aged 21 years.

83. Mary Ann wife of Lieutenant J.G. JAMES Half Pay H.M. 69th Regiment who died in this Parish 29 December 1832 in his 38th year.

84. Mr John CHILD of this Parish died 16 May 1836 aged 48 years. Julia daughter of above died 25 May 1832 in her 6th year. Elizabeth relict of above Mr John Child died 31 May 1850 aged 50 years.   84A..Josiah son of Richard and Sarah CHAPMAN born 23 May 1790 died 10 September 1790.

84B. In memory of Richard Thomas and Robert sons of Richard and Mary CHAPMAN of this Parish. Richard died _ _ April 1772 _ _ weeks. Thomas died _ _ April 1773 aged 10 weeks. Robert died _ _ February 1775 aged 3 weeks.

85. Mr Jeremiah CHAPMAN of this Parish died 25 August 1831 aged 37 years. Mary Chapman died 2 February 1880 aged 78 years.

86. Mr Richard CHAPMAN born 30 November 1745 died 16 August 1800. Also Francis TOWNSEND who was born 18 August 1824

died 19 July 1835.

87. Mrs Sarah CHAPMAN who was born 5 April 1754 and died 17 August 1827. Also Mary Oliver Chapman daughter of above born 8 February 1787 died 17 November 1805.

88. Mr Trobenius CHAPMAN of this Parish died 25 December 1840 aged 59 years. Mrs Elizabeth Chapman widow of above died 20 February 1845 aged 68 years.

89. Charlotte Swain HARDEE daughter of Mr James and Charlotte Hardee of Southwark died 16 March 1815 aged 1 years 11 months.

90. Richard Edward son of Thomas and Harriot WESTBROOK born 28 September 1859 died 2 February 1861.

91. William RIDLEY late of this Parish died 17 September 1705 aged 57 years.

92. Mr William BRASIER late of Jamaica Row Bermondsey died 6 December 1819 aged 39 years. Dear wife and children etc he left 2 infant children viz Henry Hooper and Thomas William Brasier by his wife Elizabeth.

93. Mary BRASIER wife of William Brasier of Greenhithe in this Parish died 21 August 1811 aged 31 years. Left issue 2 children, William and Edward.

94. Footstone M.A.B. 1805

95. Large low tomb: Sophia Eliza wife of Thomas Hibberds CLUETT youngest daughter of Jeremiah and Eliza BROWN died 1 December 1855 in her 22nd year.

96. Mr Thomas BROWN of Greenhithe in this Parish died 10 December 1795 aged 53 years. Mary Ann Brown daughter of Thomas and Ann Brown died 27 November 1805 aged 18 years. Also four children of above Thomas and Ann Brown, Thomas, John, Rebecca and Ann. Also Mrs Elizabeth REED wife of Mr Abraham Reed and daughter of the above Thomas Brown died 21 August 1808 aged 37 years.

97. Sarah wife of William SALE of Charing Cross, Westminster died 10 June 1816 aged 50 years. Also William their son who died in infancy. Also above William Sale died 8 August 1826 aged 61 years.

98. Sarah wife of Arthur READ died 26 July 1853 aged 37 years, [see 110]

99. Mary Ann MURRAY died 13 September 1862 aged 22 years. Charles William Lawrance Murray died 16 May 1864 aged 4 years.

100. Mrs Mary CHILD relict of Mr William Child of this Parish died 9 March 1838 aged 73 years. Mr William Child son of above died 22 May 1838 aged 52 years.

101. William CHILD late of this Parish born 11 December 1732 and died 10 November 1779. Ann Child wife of above died 12 May 1782 aged 43 years.

102. Mr William BAXTER of Greenhithe died 24 February 1856 aged 85 years. Elizabeth Baxter his wife died 18 July 1860 aged 87 years.

103. To children of Mr and Mrs SHELBOURNE late of this Parish, Mary Ann died 23 September 1823 aged 10 weeks, Maria died 27 July 1825 aged 1 year, William died 22 August 1826 aged 9 months, William Henry died 22 July 1834 aged 2 years 10 months, George died 3 October 1837 aged 2 years, Ellen died 2 November 1838 aged 7 months.

104. Here lyeth the body of Henry HARDEN died 6 July 1723 aged 68 years. Also the body of Henry Harden son of the above Henry Harden who died 8 January 1727/8 aged 33 years. Verse: Tho 'Borea's' blast and Neptunes waves. He lost us to our few. Inspite of both by God's decree. We Harbour here below where we do ride at Anchor safe with many of our Fleet (rest under ground).

105. Charles STEWART infant son of Charles and Elizabeth PULLING died 12 August 1832 (no age)

106. Mrs Hestor WESTON late wife of Mr John Weston of Greenhithe in this Parish died 10 December 1800 aged 29 years. Also John Weston son of above died in infancy. Also Ann Weston daughter of above Mr John Weston died 12 April 1810 aged 5 months.

107. Peter Cornelius van KEMPEN born in Amsterdam Holland 17 January 1796, died 21 June 1857 in his 61st year,

108. Mr Ralph WHEATLEY of this Parish died 23 March 1844 aged 66 years. Ralph Wheatley eldest son of above died 28 June 1852 aged 49 years. John Townsend Wheatley born 17 July 1808, died 5 June 1871. Sarah Fulljames Wheatley born 2 January 1813, died 8 November 1873.

109. Sarah wife of Ralph WHEATLEY of this Parish born 10 July 1777, died 22 September 1821. Mary daughter of above born 24 September 1804, died 8 November 1814. Thomas Wheatley died 3 November 1838 aged 32 years.

110. 4 footstones: R. R. 1805, E. R. 1808, A. R. 1823, A. R. 1826, [? Read of no 98 and 111]

111. Elizabeth READ, formerly of the Parish of Southfleet and late of Thames Street, Rotherhithe died 4 May 1835 aged 78 years.

112. Moses MANNING late a master and owner of a vessel from Redbridge near Southampton who died in the third fit coming down London River on 5th day of May 1832 in the (?4)9 year of his age.

113. Rib brick altar with stone top: Here lieth the body of Cook TOLLET Gent, younger son of George Tollet Esq. Commissioner of the Navy in the reigns of King William the 3rd and Queen Anne by his wife Elizabeth Cook he dyed 20 July 1738 in the forty-first year of his age. To whose memory Hannah his wife and Elizabeth his sister have placed this tombstone.

114. Mr James HIGHAM late of Greenhithe died 10 April 1817 aged 70 years. Mr Robert Higham his son died 19 June 1835 aged 47 years.

115. Mrs Sarah NETHERCOAT daughter of George and Sarah Nethercoat of this Parish died 23 July 1781 aged 20 years and 5 months.

116. Mary NETHERCOAT daughter of George and Sarah Nethercoat died 5 April 1773 in her 10th year.

117. George NETHERCOAT died 13 September 1762 aged 6 months. Ann Nethercoat died 22 October 1766 (no age).

118. Mr George NETHERCOAT yeoman late of this Parish who left behind him, his widow and 4 daughters died 8 January 1769 aged 38 years.

119. Mrs Sarah NETHERCOAT wife of Mr George Nethercoat late of this Parish died 30 August 1793 aged 68 years.

120. Mrs Martha ASHBY wife of Mr Richard Millson Ashby of Dartford died 26 May 1818 aged 53 years.

121. A large low tomb entirely covered with thick ivy.

122. William BEADLE died 23 November 1841 aged 23 years. Also Thomas SAWYER died 24 March 1852 aged 68 years.

123. Thomas BURDES of Greenhithe, formerly of Monkwearmouth Durham died 9 July 1848 aged 67 years. Margaret relict of above died 28 March 1863 aged 82 years. Also their children, viz: Edward died 10 September 1811 aged 15 months, Anne died 12 June 1821 aged 15 years, Helen died 5 October 1833 aged 21 years, Catherine died 19 October 1836 aged 28 years, Margaret the youngest and last surviving daughter and wife of William ATKINSON of Monkwearmouth, Durham died 16 May 1841 aged 26 years.

124. Monument with an urn in railings: South side: Thomas FORREST Esq died 30 December 1863 aged 93 years. Sarah Forrest wife of Thomas Forrest died 30 November 1859 aged 80 years. Richard James Forrest son of above died 7 February 1872 aged 53 years. East end: Richard Forrest died 16 February 1807 aged 38 years. Frances Forrest died 22 October 1881 aged 76 years. Ann Forrest born 24 February 1808, died 22 December 1893. North side: In the memory of Richard Forrest Esq. of Greenhithe in this Parish died 6 February 1796 aged 62 years. Mrs Sarah Forrest widow of above died 5 August 1818 aged 82 years. Allatson Forrest died 8 January 1912 aged 88 years. William Sidney Forrest died 4 February 1915 aged 94 years. West end: James Forrest son of above Mr James Forrest of this Parish died 9 May 1794 aged 3 years 6 months. *[These people owned Swan Farm, Ash, and appear in the South Ash Manor Rolls! 1878-1921 F+Z Bamping]*

125. Mr Thomas COUCHMAN of this Parish died 17 June 1820 aged 81 years. Mrs Efree Couchman wife of Mr Thomas Couchman died 20 June 1823 aged 79 years.

126. Thomas COUCHMAN eldest son of Thomas and Efree Couchman of this Parish died 8 March 1779 aged 5 years.

127. Sarah Couchman 2nd daughter of Thomas and Efree Couchman died 5 May 1781 aged 1 year.

128. Sophia COUCHMAN 4th daughter of Thomas and Efree Couchman died 14 December 1788 aged 1 year 7 months.

129. Mr Henry William Couchman died 18 September 1807 in 30th year leaving issue 3 children Eliza Selina and Thomas. Beneath this mouldering turf lies buried a tender husband and father the best of sons of brothers and of friends.

130. _ _ eli _ _ daughter of John and Ann ALEWOOD of this Parish died 20 October 1829 aged 13 years 8 months. Above Ann Alewood died 19 April 1839 aged 60 years. And her husband John Alewood many years an inhabitant of this Parish died 8 October 1862 in his 87th year.

131. To the following children of William and Sarah BROWN of this Parish Ann Maria died 10 August 1812 aged 15 months. Henry died 20 August 1816 aged 6 months. Susan died 11 November 1819 aged 15 months. Eleanor died 25 April 1825 aged 4 years 10 months. Also Francis son of John and Sarah SMITH died 17 February 1831 aged 28 years.

132. Mr William BROWN Governor of the Poor House of this Parish 27 years, during which time he filled the situation to the satisfaction of the parishioners, died regretted 5 March 1836 in his 77 Page 61year leaving issue one son William.

133. Mr John BARNETT of Mincing Lane died at Greenhithe 24 December 1861 in his 62nd year. Erected by his widow.

134. George SMITH seaman belonging to H.M.S. Hercules who was drowned at Greenhithe 26 December 1850 aged 44 years. Erected by his shipmates.

135. John MACKAY late shipmaster in Inverness died 17 May 1855 aged 55 years.

136. In railings: Thomas BRADLEY Esq. of Greenhithe died 4 September 1864 aged 83 years.

137. Thomas COUCHMAN late of this Parish, blacksmith died 28 July 1761 aged 49 years. Mary Couchman his wife died 6 September 1759 aged 47 years.

138. Large tomb in railings: North side Mr William BASSETT of Greenhithe died 28 February 1804 aged 70 years. Mrs Martha Bassett his wife died 12 November 1773 aged 34 years. Likewise James and Ann two of their children died in infancy. West end: Mrs Mary PALMER of this Parish died 10 June 1820 aged 64 years. On small cross in front of West side. Mary Catherine RUSSELL died 18 August 1865 aged 11 months. South side: Mr John Russell formerly of Manor House in this Parish late of Summer Hill Dartford died 23 November 1843 aged 73 years. Martha his widow died 1 August 1851 aged 80 years. Mr William Edward Russell of this Parish died 4 August 1859 aged 57 years. Eleanor Anastasia 2nd wife of above died 25 November 1889 aged 87 years. East end: In a vault beneath are deposited the remains of Mr Thomas GREGORY of Gravesend died 31 October 1804 aged 64 years

139. To the memory of Mary 1850 rest gone Footstones: M.J.H. 1850 L.H. 1865 O.H. 1865

140. William, son of William and Ruth COOPER died 26 October 1821 aged 8 months.

141. Ann RHOADE died 28 August 1796 aged 23 years. On right are the remains of Lydia WARD died 9 February 1811 aged 81 years.

142. Jane HICKS spinster and eldest daughter of the late John CHAMPION Esq. and Mary Charlotte CAREY his wife of the island of Guernsey who died at Greenhithe 30 August 1859 aged 68 years.

143. Ann Eliza MANTLE sister of Fanny WHATSON died 16 August 1911 aged 65 years.

144. Fanny wife of William John WHATSON died 10 January 1892 aged 52 years. Above William John Whatson died 9 December 1915 aged 78 years.

145. Mr William WATSON died 8 January 1826 in his 80th year.

146. Mr Solomon WELLS of this Parish died 23 June 1826 aged 73 years.

147. Large monument in railings at West gate: South side: Mary wife of Mr W. E. RUSSELL of the Manor House, in this Parish daughter of the late Commander T. HILL, R.N. died 27 December 1844 aged 42 years. Also William eldest son of above William

Edward and Mary Russell died 10 June 1863 aged 29 years. East end: Edward Thomas son of William Edward and Mary Russell died 6 January 1898 in his 62nd year. West side: Margaret last surviving child of the late Commander Thomas and Mary Hill died 7 March 1895 aged 90 years. North side, front: Sacred to the memory of Commander Thomas Hill R.N. of Greenhithe died 8 December 1836 aged 69 years. Mrs Mary Hill widow of above died 6 January 1862 aged 95 years. Also Lieutenant Thomas Sharp Hill R.N. son of above died at Smyrna *(Turkey)* 11 November 1845 in his 39th year.

148. Mary widow of William DICKINSON Esq. solicitor formerly of London born 25 February 1773 died at Greenhithe in this Parish 20 February 1859.

149. Emma wife of John Henry DAY died 17 April 18(?31) aged 26 years.

150. Robert W. FISHER a native of Orford in Suffolk accidentally drowned in the Thames 27 July 1865 aged 2(?4) years.

151. Rebecca wife of William GOREHAM of this Parish died 10 July 1865 aged 44 years. Harriott their infant daughter died 14 February 1851 aged 13 months Mary wife of John Goreham and mother of above William Goreham died 16 June 1859 aged 78 years. Also William Goreham died 24 March 1886 aged 67 years.

152. Mr James MOSS late of this Parish, bricklayer died 20 March 1801 aged 51 years. William Moss son of above died 15 May 1797 aged 5 weeks.

153. Footstone: J 1798 S

154. In memory of ?John SMALE[?] only child of John and Katherine Smale[?] the EGGMOUNT (?name of a ship) who died 28 May 1798 aged (?) 4 years four months. End of churchyard 24 June 1922 In the church:

155. West end of North Aisle matrix [outline] of a brass woman pedimental head dress + 2 husbands + 3 or 4. 3 sons. Eus 2 daus Nave Floor

156. Mrs Elizabeth LEFEBURE died 1 August 1826 aged 83 years. Charles Gore Lefebure died 29 July 1829 aged 82 years.

157. Rev. Charles Robert MARSHALL died 12 April 1823 aged 58 years.

158. Stone with heraldic shield at the top Mr John BAYLY died 7 February 1791 aged 65 years. Mrs Sarah Bayly wife of above died 4 November 1817 aged 86 years. Mr John Howard Bayly eldest son of above died 31 March 1824 aged 68 years. Mrs Ann STYLES 2nd daughter of above died 5 March 1831 aged 65 years. Mr James Bayly 2nd son of above died 31 July 1834 aged 76 years.

Names Index

ABBOTT 2
ALEWOOD 30
ANDREWS 3
ARLETT 8-30
ASHBY 20
ATKINSON 23
M.A.B. 4
BARNETT 33
BARTLETT 0
BASSETT 38
BAXTER 02
BAYLY 58
BEADLE 22
BLISS
BRADLEY 36
BRAMWELL 8
BRASIER 92, 3
Bray 7
BROWN 95, 96, 131, 132 BURDES 23
BY 9
CAREY 42
Cartwright 9
CHALLIS 9
CHAMPION 42
CHAPMAN 1, 5, 84A+B, 5-88
CHILD 4, 100,
01 CLUETT
5 COLYER
8 Cook
13 COOPER
40 COSSART
0 COUCHMAN
25-129, 137 CURTIS 22 DAVIDSON
1 DAY
49 DICKINSON
48 DONNE 52-54

Drew 46
DURLING 70, 72
Edmeades 25
EDWARDS 32
ELAND 2
EVEREST 62
FARMER-FRANCIS 79
FELDWICK 78
FIELDER 74
FISHER 150
FORREST 124
FRANCIS 79
FULLJAMES 69, 108
GOREHAM 151
GOSTLING 64
GRAY 74
GREGORY 138
M.J.H. 139
HALL 41
HARDEE 89
HARDEN 104
HARDS 15
HARE 34
HAYES 76
HENDEN 35
HEWITT 59
Hibberds 95
HICKS 142
HIGHAM 114
HILL 57, 147
HOADLEY 51
HOLDAWAY 81
HOLLAND 63
Hooper 92
HORLOCK 75
HURST 1
INGALL 46
JAMES 82
JAY 62
KEMPEN, van 107

KING 62
KINGSLAND 62
LAVENDER 16
LAWRANCE 35, 99
LEFEBURE 156
MACKAY 135
MANNING 112
MANTLE 143
MARSHALL 157
MARTIN 15, 15a
MASON 67
McBEATH 26
Millson 120
Mitford 48
MORRIS 39
MOSS 152
MUNN 23, 24
MURRAY 99
MUSGROVE 77
NETHERCOAT 115-119
PALMER 138
PARSONS 61
PIRKINS 80
POWSEY 9-14
PRIME 31
PULLING 105
PUSTWELL 42
R. R.110
READ 98, 111
RHOADE 141
RICHARDSON 60
RIDLEY 91
RIXSON 7, 13
RUSSELL 138, 147
J S 153
SALE 98
SAWYER 122
Sharp 147
SHELBOURNE 103
SHEPHERD 37

SIMMONS 75
SMALE[?] 154
SMALL 8, 45, 65, 66
SMITH 131, 134
SOWTON 82
STEVENS 62
STEWART 105
STYLES 158
Swain 89
SWETTENHAM 30
Tankerville 46
TOLHURST 25
TOLLET 113
TOWNSEND 86, 108
van KEMPEN 107
VITOU 61
VOGAN 43
M.A.W. 21
W.W. 21
WALLIS 17
WARD 141
WARE 3, 4, 5, 6
WARNER 73
WATERS 38
WATSON 145
WATTS 18
WELLS 146
WEST 44
WESTBROOK 90
WESTON 105
WHATSON 143, 144
WHEATLEY 108, 109
WHISKIN 58
WHITEHEAD 47
WILKS 40
WILLIAMS 18
WOODWARD 36
WOOTTON 56

Swanscombe Cemetery

The Lych Gate c1930

The Swanscombe Burial Ground was opened in 1885 and purchased at a cost of £493; the first burial being Ada Ayra Cleaves on 3 April 1887.
Within the Cemetery is a small but charming chapel built in 1905.

1910

1910

The well maintained 4.5,acre site features an avenue of mature trees, shrubs and rose beds with an informal lay out.

Entrance at the Swanscombe Street end is via a traditional lychgate opposite the historical St Peter & St Paul's Church.

There are 16 war graves and Henry Stopes, the father of Marie Stopes, buried in 1902, can be found in the cemetery

Photographs of the Lychgate The Chapel and the Cemetery 2011

All Saints' Church, Galley Hill 1894-1990

All Saints Church Galley Hill 1905

It would seem strange to anyone these days, but why All Saint's Church, was built was mainly due to the "Cement Works" as for some reason in 1881 it agreed that the formation of a new parish would be created. And so 1883, The Parish of All Saints, Swanscombe, comprising the Galley Hill Ward of the Urban District of Swanscombe. Out of a part of the ancient parish of St Peter & Paul, Swanscombe. The Galley Hill Ward started at the bottom of the Hill just past the Ebbsfleet Football Club,(or where the Black Eagle pub used to be) up to the George and Dragon, and Down to the Entrance to the Old White Works. This I am sure was the desire of the proprietors of the Portland cement factory by J B White and son's to promote the spiritual welfare of the workers for the industry and their livelihood. The first Church built in 1882, was a modest sized building made of Iron, and was later used as a church hall. And so on Wednesday 11th July 1894 at 7pm, a service was held for the laying of the Foundation Stone.

The First Vicar of the Parish was the Rev H Russell Wakefield (afterwards Lord Bishop of Birmingham). The Parish Church of All Saints, built to the design of the late Norman Shaw, R.A., was the gift of three members of the White family: Leedham White, John Bazley White, and Frederick Anthony White. It was consecrated on July 23rd,1895 by the late Rt Rev R T Davidson, the then Bishop of Rochester, and then, Archbishop of Canterbury. The Church is notable not only for its beauty of its architecture and furnishings, but also for the art treasures it contains. Which include oil paintings by Caracci, Albertinelli, and other old masters: a Litany desk fashioned from a fifteenth century tabernacle from the hand of the late Stirling Lee. R.A., All gifts of the surviving founder, Mrs F A White, to whom the Parish owes a debt of deepest gratitude.

Artist impression of the not yet built Church 1893   *All Saints Galley Hill Interior c1920*

All Saint's Church, Galley Hill, 1894. This photograph appears to show Galley Hill Church shortly after the current building was constructed in 1894: the church's fabric appears to be very crisp and new. All Saint's was originally a corrugated iron construction on the opposite side of London Road and was created as a separate church parish from the original parish church of Swanscombe (Saint's Peter and Paul) in 1883. The huge growth of the Galley Hill area over the previous 30-40 years meant that what was a country lane to Swanscombe Street was now a busy bustling community which became the High Street we know today. Two county constabulary policemen are standing left of the entrance gate, with the Alma public house in the High Street (belonging to the Dartford Brewery Company) and the roofs of the houses in Orchard Street in the background. Orchard Street was completely redeveloped in the early 1950s and was one of the first slum clearance schemes in Swanscombe.
(From Christoph Bull "Swanscombe in old picture postcards" 2005)

Rev James Thomas Christie and Choir 1884-90

Clergy and guests at All Saint's Church, Galley Hill, This photograph was taken on 23 July 1895 when All Saint's Church had been completed and was being dedicated. The original corrugated iron building standing opposite was now used as a church house meeting room and for parish council meetings. The Bishop of Rochester, the Right Reverend Randall Thomas Davidson – bishop from 1891 till 1895, later Archbishop of Canterbury 1903-1928 – is seated with his mortarboard; mitres were seen as too papist for the Church of England at this time. To the bishop's right is Rev.Arthur F.E. Owen, vicar 1890-1900; and to his left is Canon Murray, Rural Dean and Rector of Stone. The other guests are local worthies including members of the White Family, Cement Works owners and major church benefactors. The gentleman who is fifth from the left standing is John Bazley White (1848-1927), along with Leedham White (1838-1905) 7th from left, and Frederick Anthony White (1842-1933) 12th from left. These men had enormous influence in Swanscombe because of their wealth and status as major employers and they saw the church as providing spiritual and moral guidance to their army of workers. *(From Christoph Bull "Swanscombe in old picture postcards" 2005)*

ALL SAINTS', ✝ SWANSCOMBE.

Special Evening Service

AFTER THE

Laying of the Foundation Stone of the New Church.

WEDNESDAY, 11th JULY, 1894, at 7 p.m.

The Shortened Service for Evening Prayer

WILL BE AS FOLLOWS:—

PROCESSIONAL HYMN, No. 1, on the next page.

| SENTENCES. | CONFESSION. | OUR FATHER, &c. |
| DEARLY BELOVED, &c. | ABSOLUTION. | VERSICLES. |

SPECIAL PSALM, 103, No. 2.
1ST SPECIAL LESSON, I CHRONICLES XXII.

MAGNIFICAT, No. 3.
2ND SPECIAL LESSON, REVELATION XXI, VERSES 1—7 AND 19—27.

NUNC DIMITTIS, No. 4.
APOSTLE'S CREED AND THE FOLLOWING PRAYERS:

COLLECT FOR THE 7TH SUNDAY AFTER TRINITY. PRAYER FOR THE ROYAL FAMILY.
COLLECT FOR PEACE. PRAYER FOR THE CLERGY AND PEOPLE.
COLLECT AGAINST ALL PERILS. GENERAL THANKSGIVING.
PRAYER FOR THE QUEEN'S MAJESTY. PRAYER OF ST. CHRYSOSTOM.

THE GRACE.

HYMN, No. 5.
SERMON BY THE REV. CANON POLLOCK.

HYMN, No. 6.
BENEDICTION.

RECESSIONAL HYMN, No. 7.

CADDEL & SON, PRINTERS, KING STREET, GRAVESEND.

Order of Service Laying of the Foundation Stone 1893

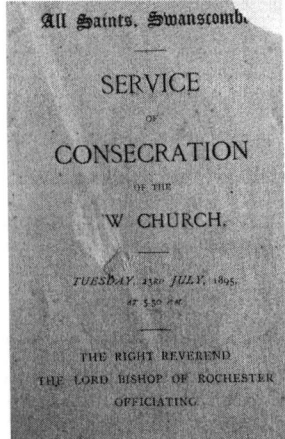
Conseccration Sevice 1895

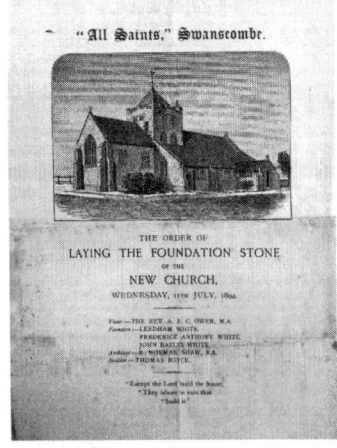
Full Foundation Stone Service 1894

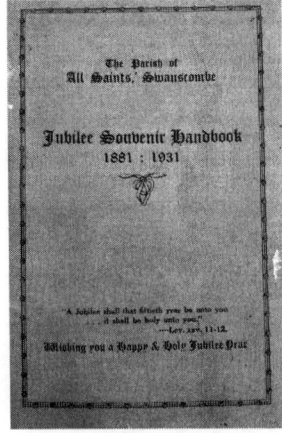
Jubilee Handbook 1931

Church Images

All Saints Galley Hill Interior 1932

Interior of All Saint's, Galley Hill, circa 1935. This view shows the well-provided for church, which had so much help in its foundation from the White Family – owner of Swanscombe Cement Works. The architect was Richard Norman Shaw (1831-1912); a stained glass window was by Christopher Whall (1849-1921), a leader in the revival of post-medieval stained glass. The church was largely built with the financial aid given by Messrs. Leedham, John Bazley and Frederick Anthony White. It contained several art treasures including two paintings: a crucifixion by Iacopo da Carucci (1494-1556) and a Madonna with two children by Mariotto Albertinelli (1474-1515), a litany desk made from a sixteenth century Spanish tabernacle and an eighteenth-century candelabrum. The treasures were removed to Saint Peter and Paul's Church when All Saint's was declared redundant by the Church of England in 1971, but some have been subsequently sold. In 1990 the empty building was tastefully converted into flats. *(*From Christoph Bull "Swanscombe in old picture postcards" 2005).

All Saints Galley Hill & Tram 1925

A Slow End

The sad and slow end for this much loved church, is in no coincidence, linked as its creation to the decline and closure of the White Works. The last incumbant The Rev Montague J.Cox bachelor Vicar of All Saints, Galley Hill, lives in a 14 room vicarage next to which a terrace of large houses is in process of being developed. Dust from the local cement works lies everywhere like pumis after a volcano, and altogether it is a depressing sight,

Mr Cox whose comes from the charming Sussex village of Chailey. He is a countryman at heart, hoping one day to find a little cottage with green fields around, and no cement dust.

Galley Hill's vicar is the longest serving incumbent in the Gravesend Deanery, he came here in September 1932, and is also the second longest serving priest in the Rochester diocese.

The Patron of the living when he was appointed was Mr Frederick White, one of the founders of the cement works in North Kent. Now it is his grandson Major Jeremy White. In World War I Mr Cox was in the Church Army, helping to run a recreation room for the troops in Egypt. While on the way out his ship was torpedoed 90 miles of Crete.

Mr Cox will soon have completed 41 years in the Ministry having been ordained in Lichfield Cathedral in 1926 after studying at Lichfield Theological College.

Life on the tough side.
Church life at Galley Hill, Mr Cox finds to be on the tough side. "It is a rapidly shrinking parish with hardly any new development" he said "In ten years we have lost 500 parishioners and a wedding at the church a few days ago was the first since last July. "We are surrounded by chalk pits. The youngsters leave when they get married and so Galley Hill is becoming a parish of elderly people".

"Our Sunday school has gone and the need for more church workers is great. I am the church treasurer which should be a layman's job. "I am afraid Galley Hill is a noisy dusty area for which no one cares". Among the Vicars of Galley Hill have been two who later became Bishops, Dr Russell Wakefield, and Hamilton Lang. The Father of Miss Phyilis Bottome, the novelist, was one of the vicars and his daughter wrote about Galley Hill.

Mr Cox spent some happy years from 1936 to 1943 as a member of Swanscombe Council and was chairman of the health committee. " I enjoyed the work" he said " and was sorry to call it a day". With advancing years he is naturally thinking of the time when he will give up the living which he has held longer than any of his predecessors, but at the moment he has no definite plans. It is possible that Mr Cox will be the last Vicar of All Saints' Galley Hill. When he goes the living could well be amalgamated with that of Swanscombe

The Rev M J Cox

The Last page in the Baptism Records 25th May 1971

Article written in 1969

And so it was that on the 25th May 1971 Rev David Ash declared the Church "Redundant"

All Saints c1930

Appointed Vicar of Swanscombe

(Printed in the Chronicle 28.8.1925)

The Rev. E.L.M. Allen

The many friends whom the Rev. Ernest L M Allen has made since he came to Bromley Parish Church as Curate in November, 1923, will be sorry to know that he will shortly be leaving them, having, been appointed to take charge of All Saints' at Swanscombe. They will however, be glad to feel that in this promotion to a more responsible sphere of work, Mr Allen is receiving recognition for the very solid and useful work he has done, not only in Bromley, but in other parishes with which he was associated before coming to Bromley. The Vicar of Bromley himself the Rev. Canon J K Wilson describes Mr Allen as "a reliable and scholarly teacher of high ideals." He has always been appreciated both in the pulpit and outside the church and his special work in connection with the children's Catechism at St. Mark's and the Children's Temperance and Missionary Guild at the Church at the Church Institute has been immensely satisfactory.

Swanscombe is one of the numerous "cement" towns in the Thames Valley, and possesses a population almost entirely composed of cement workers to the number of 3000, and has, says Mr Allen, "a beautiful little church, day schools, and a Sunday School of 600 children, and in addition it has a Bible Class of about a 100 children and extraordinary number for a town so small."

Mr Allen will leave Bromley accompanied by the good wishes and congratulations of all with whom his work has brought him into contact. He is well equipped to take charge of an independent sphere, and the Church of Swanscombe should derive new impetus and benefit from his ministrations. He is a B.A. and B.D. of London University, and before being ordained he was trained at Leeds Clergy School. He has served in curacies at St Paul's, Haggerston, Holy Trinity, Guildford, Holy Trinity Eltham, and was also vice principle of the Missionary College of Dorchester, and for four years secretary of Canterbury and Rochester Diocesan Church of England Temperance Society.

AN IMAGINATIVE PLAN TO TURN DESERTED CHURCH INTO FLATS

Lovely old building is set for new lease of life

by Nick Antonovics

A DESERTED church is to get a new lease of life thanks to an enterprising man from Greenhithe.

All Saints Church, Swanscombe, has been closed for more than 10 years, but now the listed building is to be converted into 14 flats and maisonettes.

The idea for the project has come from Stephen O'Sullivan, a builder from Knockhall Road, Greenhithe.

In use again

Both he and former Dartford councillor Paddy Melvin wanted to see the church in use again.

So Mr O'Sullivan formed a company and commissioned Kent architect Chris Anderson to come up with a design.

Mr Anderson, who trained at the Thames Polytechnic now based in Dartford, said the unique nature of the building proved his greatest challenge.

"I have designed blocks of flats before, but with the church each had to be built to fit into the existing structure."

Interior stonework and arches are to be retained in the design which has already got the backing of Dartford councillors.

But English Heritage must also approve the plans because of the church's important history.

It was built in 1894 by Richard Norman Shaw, famous for his revival of a traditional style in architecture.

While other Victorians were building their churches from brick, he chose to use flint and stone.

Consequently, All Saints has the appearance of a 15th rather than 19th century building.

The church was paid for by three members of the Whyte family, whose names are commemorated on plaques inside and outside the walls.

After starting as Church of England, in its last few years All Saints became the Catholic Our Lady of Carmel.

But it will be at least two years before the church begins its new life as flats.

Although Mr Anderson is confident the design will be accepted, he said: "I should think it will be two years until people can move in."

English Heritage said it could not comment while the matter was being discussed.

Whether present-day parishioners will be able to afford to buy flats is also not known.

Mr O'Sullivan would not say how much he paid for the building, bought from the diocese of Southwark, and would make no predictions on how much thelats would eventually cost.

But with its novelty value and stunning views over the river, there is no reason why the flats shouldn't become the area's ultimate des res.

● Architect Chris Anderson goes over his plans inside All Saints Church. Picture by Kevin Coombs KA7826/9

A New life 1990

---

6 Extra, January 19, 1990 (G)

Designer church awaits 14 flat plan approval

A FAMOUS old church may become holy homes if plans for conversion to 14 flats are accepted.

The future of All Saints Church, Swanscombe, a grade II listed building of special architectural interest, lies in the hands of the Environment Secretary.

Tunbridge Wells architect Chris Anderson has produced a design which preserves the character of the church and has the backing of Dartford Borough Council.

The 97-year-old church on Galley Hill has been neglected for several years. But the unusual design of leading 19th century architect, Richard Shaw, can still be appreciated.

Shaw was a follower of cult designer William Morris and art nouveau flourishes are still to be seen inside the church. Ornate carvings and curved window arches can be admired on the outside.

Council planners believe the proposed design will protect Shaw's basic ideas even though renovation will destroy most of his interior touches.

English Heritage has been consulted about the plan which is being promoted by MK Developments of Tunbridge Wells.

Architect Chris Anderson's design, above, preserves the character of the existing church. Below, All Saint's Church as it looks today, originally the design of 19th Century architect Richard Shaw

Shop gutted by fire

A FIRE which gutted the first floor of a Dartford shop is thought to have been started by arsonists.

A blaze broke out at 4.15 am at the Handyman store and police had to close off the road as three fire pumps from Dartford took nearly three hours to douse the flames. Firemen had to wear breathing apparatus because of the thick smoke.

All Saints c1930

All Saints as Flats 2011

Chapter 4
White Works
Cement Industry 1825-1974
Extracts by Timothy Guy
Blue Circle Group

White Works Cement Industry 1825-1974

For those people reading the book, most of them would have had a family member who had at some point worked at the White Works at the bottom of Craylands Lane.

Swanscombe White Works 1909

If there is one person who changed the fortunes and indeed the landscape of Swanscombe that person is, James Frost of Finchley. He established himself at the works at Swanscombe in the year 1825 and became the first maker and producer of artificial cement in the London District. He took out patents for 'British Cement' in 1822 and 1823, the material being virtually the same as that named by Aspidin in1824 as Portland Cement, which was basically an improved ground hydraulic lime. He ran the works until 1833 when his interest passed to Mr J B White Senior. Who was a partner in the firm of Francis, White and Francis. This partnership continued until 1837 when the works were made over entirely to Messrs J B White and Son.

Photo:of Mr I C Johnson with members of the White Family on his 100th Birthday. And examples of early packaging for export and delivery, Jute sacks and wooden barrels which were all filled by hand.

Some time after 1840, White's refined Frost's process and succeeded in making a product which they also called "Portland Cement" Mr I C Johnson, whom the old Johnsons works was named, was largely responsible for the development of this cement. Some years later, Johnson described how he was unable to find out what Aspdin was doing, but his own experiments finally resulted in a formula that produced a cement almost identical to that of Aspdin.

George Frederick White became senior partner with John Bazley Jnr. When their father, Mr J B White retired in 1844. He had a thorough understanding of the possibilities of Portland cement and is believed to have been one of the originators of testing cement using briquettes, the forerunners of today's cube test. At the Great Exhibition in Hyde Park in 1851,

Swanscombe Chalk Quarry in the early days

In 1874, an attempt was made to close the works by legal proceedings on the grounds that 'the smoke from the works caused a nuisance' was prejudicial to health and likely to deteriorate the value of the surrounding property'. This attempt resulted in large demonstrations and meetings of the working men in support of the works and expressing dissatisfaction at the proceedings. In October the action was withdrawn and the following notice displayed in the works: Messrs J B White Bros are glad to announce that the prosecution has been withdrawn. They take this opportunity of expressing to all persons in their employ their deep sense of sympathy and kind feeling which has been manifested on their behalf.

George Frederick White took a great in the well-being of the work people and among other things provided a school for the education of their families. He retired in 1882 and was followed by Frederick Anthony White who became the first Chairman of APCM on its formation in 1900

Locomotive 'Millbank' C1879   Thames Sailing Barges at Swanscombe Wharf

by APCM, no less than 16 rotary kilns were installed. These kilns were 6ft 5in diameter and 80ft in length, This new works suffered a reverse in 1904, when the river bank burst causing extensive flooding.

Three new kilns being installed in 1928

The 1914-18 war produced problems, most of the men joining the forces. Their place was taken by women who not only worked in the cooperage (most of the cement still being packed in barrels), but also did the most of the labouring work.

The war over, there was a steady rise in demand for cement until the 1920's when requirements began to diminish. Efforts were made in many fields to reduce the production costs, not only in the mechanical field, but also in the quarrying methods. The whole plant was rebuilt and three new kilns commissioned (above) by the end of 1929. In 1931-32 a new plant was built to produce white cement – Snowcrete. By 1935 there were eight rotary kilns in operation.

Rotary Kilns Firing Floor 1911

Many men who were territorial were in camp with Major Dawson when the 1939-45 war was declared, Many others joined up and served in all parts of the world. The works did not take any direct hits from air raids despite heavy bombing in the area, and production for the war effort continued at full pressure. Mr D Nye managed the works during this period handing over to R V Beal in 1947

Jute sack filling c1900

A Period of re-organisation and clearing up then started. The war having delayed any development. Production reached a high level within a few years, the many improvements contributing to a greatly improved production figures, Quarrying once more became difficult due to problems related to removal of topsoil but were overcome by the introduction of more powerful earthmoving machinery and a belt conveyor one mile long to take the soil away.

Mr J R Hawes continued this period of consolidation when in 1952 he replaced Mr Beal on his appointment as Southern Area Manager. Works production was once again stopped on 31st January 1953 by extensive flooding from the River Thames. By a superhuman effort on everyone's part, production was resumed by 9th February 1953.

An Atkinson Steam Lorry   Flooding opposite Swanscombe Canteen 1953

Swanscombe has always been noted for a progressive outlook and despite its age, the works have been consistently improved over the years. In recent years major alterations have been taken place including the construction of a new whiting plant and many improvements to the production of the Groups 'Special Products manufactured of Mr C H Cronkshaw, 1959-1967, Mr J Templar, 1967-1968, Mr T Thompson, 1968-1970, and from 1970 to 1974 by Mr D Workman.

The transportation of cement from the Swanscombe factory was quite complex, Early on Frost laid a railway line across the marsh to a wharf on the Thames, this probably accounts for the curious 3ft 5 and Half inch gauge with the wheel flanges running on the outside. This rail was not replaced until 1929. The line would have commenced with horse haulage, the great bulk of cement being dispatched from the wharf in the picturesque Thames Barges. It is not known when the first locomotives were introduced but an entry in old account book shows trains 'Ironhorse' and 'Millbay' being rebuilt in 1916, the trains dating from 1882 and 1884 respectively. The same account book has entries in 1917 for 'Toronto' and 'Terry' two of the many horses in use at the works. It is about this time that road transport were being used.

The fully restored Loco "Swanscombe" and the "Swanscombe working in 1930 at the quarry

The Entrance to the White Works Swanscombe Cement Factory c1900,
and the house where John Blazley White, Lived.

A Visit to White's Works Swanscombe, March 1877

The works lie between Greenhithe and Northfleet, in the parish of Swanscombe, and were we believe, commenced in a much humbler form by Mr. Frost in 1823, from whom were purchased by Mr.White in 1833; attaining their present size by a steady development of the cement trade both at home and abroad.

The Approach from the river slope, past Ingress Abbey, shows the whole of the works, snugly ensconced in a hollow, from which eighteen tall chimneys stood up into the sky. The upper air around the spot, is at times somewhat smoky; but below, or on approach very little is perceptible. Arrived at the entrance, we are soon busily occupied in keeping a watchful eye, with a view to personal security, on the loaded cars, which shoot to and fro over the many interlaced railways leading to the river and about the works. Our Guide today will be Mr. Glover the manager whose technical knowledge render him an excellent and moreover a good companion.

Winding our way through the kiln passages, with which the works are tunneled everywhere, in a rabbit burrow fashion, behold us standing at the foot of a cliff, which is cut well back inland, and presents a perpendicular scarp, from70 to 80 feet deep. Thence the freshly cut chalk, snowy white in the light, dimly blue in the shadow, is being cut at mid-level, and lowered into wagons by means of slots cut in the cliff, the passages and apparatus going under the name of mills. The Material is then conveyed to the mixing mills, with any flints which may have got through, as these latter are by now means looked on as desirable accompaniments, and so are consequently picked out by hand. The portion excavated forms a large pit, some 20 acres in extent; the entire works encompasses 60 or 70 acres.

Before we leave to follow the chalk cars and wagons, we must give a last look at the fine new Hoffman kiln, which is now almost finished, and occupies a central position in the pit. It is a large oblong structure 250 feet by 90, with 16 compartments, through which flames are drawn off by a colossal shaft, 260 feet high. The structure was built under the supervision of Mr. Glover. Passing on to the chalk cars, which have, no doubt, been waiting for us too long, we ascend a few steps and find ourselves gazing down into a large circular receptacle, in which, with hideous and discordant clangour, the chalk we have seen, is being mixed with the other requisite the clay by a revolving wheel furnished with tines; the passage of which latter over the floor amongst the stray flints which have found their way in, causes the noise, which is to say the least, considerable. These same flints afford and interesting illustrations of the formation of pebbles, due to the constant grinding and rubbing, rolling about for two to three days, and incessant friction against each other and the times, they become changed from the well known large angular flints of chalk, into most respectably polished pebbles. Mingled with a little of the mixture in which they lie, they form an excellent concrete. The clay lies beside us; it is an alluvial deposit from the estuaries and creeks of the Medway, and is of a dark grey colour. It has moreover, a greasy soapy feel, suggestive of a large percentage of alumina.

The wash mill or mixing machine we were examing , which is one of many is worked by a compound engine of 250 horsepower and the "slurry' as the grey slushy looking mixture is called, after flowing through into an adjoining house, is lifted by elevating wheels to an upper story, whence it is passed between horizontal milestone and comminuted to a further extent by a process of rapid revolution until ready to be pumped away. As eight pairs of these stones here combine to produce a deafening roar, we are only two delighted to pass on to the next point of interest, the engine room. We learn that there are three other of these mill houses with six stones each. The engine also drives a machine for drawing the tramlines up the inclines. The mixture is drawn through flues beneath and around the drying floor, on which the compound flows in a thick treacally stream from the pipes. It speedily solidifies and cracks in every direction; until a sufficient dryness having been obtained the stuff is removed in masses about a foot square. It has now the appearance of a number of fire bricks fused together, and is vesicular in structure, Mr. Glover informs me that it has now acquired a new name, and that the old one must no be heard of no more, so we will now follow the "dried slip" as it is now called, on its way to the kilns. It is now put into barrows with a sufficient quantity of coke and burned at a nearly white heat. The product is semi-vitrified and of a dark grey colour. Once more the name is changed, and we now have to deal with the product now known as "clinker".

In this last operation, the material has undergone a great chemical change. Originally we had a material mixture of chalk, which is almost entirely carbonate of lime, and clay, which is called silicate of alumina. At the intense heat to which the mixture is subjected in the kilns, the lime parts with its carbonic acid, which with a varying amount of carbonic-oxide and watery vapour passes up the tall shaft. It then unites with a portion of silicic acid in the clay, so as to form a double silicate of lime and alumina with an excess of caustic lime. It only now remains to grind up the contents of the kiln, for which purpose a quantity of the crude material is transferred to steam powered crushers, The product is then raised by chain elevators to a series of smaller mills, whose rapidly revolving stones subject it to a still further process of attrition. The chamber is filled with a dun coloured cloud, and the floor is deeply covered with the fine particles; but, though the visitor speculates as to irritated lungs and blocked air-cells, the workman one and all, seem healthy enough and assure us that the experience no inconvenience. Below, the process of packing, is being carried on the conveyor belt, the powder passes down a shoot and is then slid into sacks and casks. It is then allowed to cool, for in the process of the final grinding, it has attained a temperature of 140 degrees or even more. It is so fine that 95 per cent passes through a sieve having 2,500 meshes to the square inch. This concludes the details of the manufacturing process.

View of the locomotives pulling wagons c1910

Besides the tram cars and inclines, there are 5 little locomotives (above) busily puffing and drawing loads varying from 30 to 60 tonnes. For the repairs, which the cars sometimes require there is a "Locomotive Hospital" maintenance shed, in which we find five to six men very hard at work fixing and repairing. The engines have also their place to park in case of accident, and in the engine factory we see powerful drills, laths at work replacing broken guides parts. In the adjoining smithy are a number of forges, all worked by Giant Vaporifer. Ahead is a steam hammer, and on the one side are small but powerful wind furnaces with crucibles and tongs, for any minor brass or iron castings that may be required. We are inclined to think it is time to cry "Hold enough" but no, not even yet is the end in sight. We now reach the carpenters shop, with its distinct lathes and appliances, and now we enter the cooperage. Any wonder we might have had, as to where the thousands of casks about the works came from, vanishes at once. The staves are first shown us in the rough quite unshaped, and to all intents and purposes, mere pieces of board. The cask heads lie round us in hundreds of piles. How are they fashioned into such symmetrical curves?. Surely by some slow and tedious process. But no! We are to be shown the making the tops and bottoms, all at once, and in an instant. Six of these rough boards are put into a circular grip. A handle is turned by a small boy, and we stand aloof for a moment. There is a whir of wheels, a building shower of shavings and fragments for three or four seconds, the machinery is stopped, and there are our cask head and bottom complete. Now for the starves. The same marvelous ingenuity has not failed here. The contracting cooper Mr Hewitt shows us, with just pride an apparatus he has invented, which fashions each staves. The same marvelous ingenuity has not failed here, the cooper Mr.Hewitt shows me a machine which he invented, which fashions each stave without risk of injury. It will fashion 60 staves a minute.

Looking at the present and past condition of this centre of human ingenuity and energy, not only as a whole, but in its smallest detail, we can see the secret of its success. Steady, plodding perseverance at the head, and a readiness to further the ideas and suggestions of the everyday workforce, have borne their fruit in the conception and consummation of the schemes, by which this vast establishment has attained its size.

White Works Swansombe 1906

A Photograph of the same site today 2011

The White Works Swanscombe Founders

Top left: John Bazley White, senr. (1784-1867). Top right: John Bazley White, J.P., junr. (1814-1893). Middle left: George Frederick White (1816-1898). Middle right: Frederick Anthony White, F.S.A. (1842-1933). Bottom left: Leedham White, D.L. (1838-1905). Bottom right: John Bazley White, J.P., D.L., M.P. (1848-1927).

George Frederick White 1816-1898

Isaac Charles Johnson 1811-1911

Arial View of the White Works c1960

Entrance To the White Works Swanscombe c1957

View of the entrance to the Kent Kraft Industrial Estate 2011
(Any Trace of the Grand old works all but gone)
The White Works at Swanscombe London Road was closed down in November 1990

Swanscombe Wharf

If you walk around Swanscombe Peninsular you will eventually come to what was once the cement works wharf where all the ships were loaded with the end product from White Works up to Blue Circle. All that's left now is the wharf itself, but once was full of crains and lifting equipment.

© Ernie's Railway Archive

© Ernie's Railway Archive

Swanscombe Wharf 2014

Swanscombe Wharf 2014

© Ernie's Railway Archive

Blue Circle

in the 1920s the company's main brand name – Blue Circle – began to be used informally for the company itself. But it was not until 1978 that the UK company name was officially changed from APCM Ltd to Blue Circle Industries PLC.

The company gradually built up a competence in the technical aspects of low-cost cement manufacture, and installed many new plants during the period 1950-1970, using its own specifications. It also sold manufacturing and plant-installation turnkey consultancy.

The company faltered following the 1970s energy crisis. The company's UK capacity reached its peak of 13 million tonnes per annum in 1973, and ultimately fell to half that level. Simultaneous world-wide contraction of markets lead to severe retrenchment. In the 1980s, major overseas investments were sold out, notably the by-then very large Mexican operation. The Mexican plants became incorporated in the Cemex group, which is now the world's third largest cement manufacturer. This was followed by several failed attempts at diversification, which failed to enhance investor confidence. In the late 1990s, the company again attempted to expand its cement operations geographically, this time in cut-throat competition with other large companies.

The logo we all grew up to know, the Blue Circle Cement Bags

Blue Circle 1968 Foden Tank LorryBlue Circle 2001 ERF Tank Lorry

Company taken over

In 2001, the company, now shrunk to sixth largest worldwide, was bought by the French company Lafarge. Lafarge thus became the world's largest cement manufacturer. "Blue Circle" currently (2008) remains Lafarge's cement brand name in the UK.

Images Of The Old Works

The above four photographs are the installation of kiln no 4 at White Works by Len Todd

1950

1970

1970

1970

Cement Works Railways

By C.G.Down written in 1966

Swanscombe cement works, the largest of the many A.P.C.M. cement works in North Kent, has seven 0-4-0 saddle tanks to work the considerable traffic. Six were built by Hawthorn Leslie (four in 1928, one in 1929 and one in 1935) and the last by Robert Stephenson & Hawthorns in 1948. All seven are painted green with the running number on each side of the tank. There are no diesels; the one tried could not manage the poor track and was continually "sitting down". There is no prospect of having any until money can be spared for relaying several miles of track.

The works can be divided for convenience into three areas. The first two are old chalk pits, dug each side of the main road, while the third contains the line to the workings. The first area is bisected by a private road with the cement works proper on one side. On the other side is the single road engine shed and works, and also an awning over one track where engines stand when not in use. A single line runs past the works, and across the marshy countryside to the jetty on the river Thames.

Another line runs across the road and winds its way around the main works until entering a tunnel under the main road. This brings it to the second old pit, where are situated two unloading tips for arriving trains. As can be seen from the map, a connection to British Railways struggles up and round the side of the pit. (Sand all over the rails shows the severity of the climb.) On the opposite side of the pit, another single line dips downwards into a tunnel under BR, a road and the connecting line, and emerges into a long, deep and wide cutting. There are two passing loops on the way to the workings, of which one has watering facilities, and another tunnel, and a high footbridge.

Locomotive No.7 en route from the quarry. (D. Trevor Rowe).

Locomotive No.3 taking water. (D. Trevor Rowe).

At the middle pit, an arriving train runs above one of the two tips, and backs down on to the tip. When the end wagon is on the tip, the wagons are braked, and the locomotive is uncoupled so that it can go up to the end of the line to obtain coal and water.

The tips are similar to mechanical coaling plants on B.R. and deal with one wagon at a time. As each wagon is unloaded, it runs along the siding by gravity, until the train is reformed at the other end of the loop. The locomotive then comes back and couples onto the same end as before. The next train brings the single line tablet which is hung on a hook on a post. The first train collects the tablet and then goes down to the workings, the locomotive propelling the wagons.

I spent some time around the footbridge, photographing the trains, which passed at frequent intervals. The maximum speed was about 20m.p.h., but trains lurched terribly, due to the poor track. When the track deteriorates so much as to necessitate its replacement, diesels will doubtless be purchased. From the opinion of many of the men to whom I spoke, however, steam should retain its supremacy for some time to come.

Memories of an Industrial Railway at Swanscombe

By: Mr Stuart Bare retired steam locomotive service engineer of White's Works Pit, Swanscombe, A.P.C.M. Ltd, given on the 23/3/1968 and 8/6/1968.

Mr Bare worked for the Associated Portland Cement Manufacturers Ltd., for 50 years in servicing locomotives and other equipment. His father and grandfather also worked at the pits. It was his grandfather bought the first locomotive from Plymouth for use at Swanscombe Works. Steam locomotives were also made for White's Works at the company's Greenhithe Engineering Works. Many horses and barriers were used by the works when he was a young man in 1910.

White's Pit, Swanscombe Works, Galley Hill, used a narrow gauge which is about 3 feet railway track, until about 1920 when the standard gauge "4ft 8 half inches" was used.

Swanscombe Works had its own cooperage depot, and generated its own gas "made from sawdust waste from barrel making" but this proved too dangerous, and electricity from coal fired boilers. The works had a farrier, toolsmith, and five blacksmiths under a charge-hand blacksmith, and a cast iron and brass foundry. Horse drawn wagons would take injured workman to a doctor or hospital. Flints separated from the chalk in the wash mills were then a by product useless to the cement industry so were sold very cheaply for local building purposes.

In Swanscombe Wood Clay was dug for making cement, and before about 1921 was transported by locomotive until a pipeline enabled it to be pumped to the works. The locomotives used had vertical boilers and ran a narrow gauge track, they comprised of "Rapid","Swift", and "Alert", and were built at the company's Northfleet Engineering Works. At Swanscombe Wood, owing to its inaccessible position, the company had a self contained gas making plant and blacksmith's forge.

Mr Stuart Bare 1968

Locomotive No 1 at Swanscombe

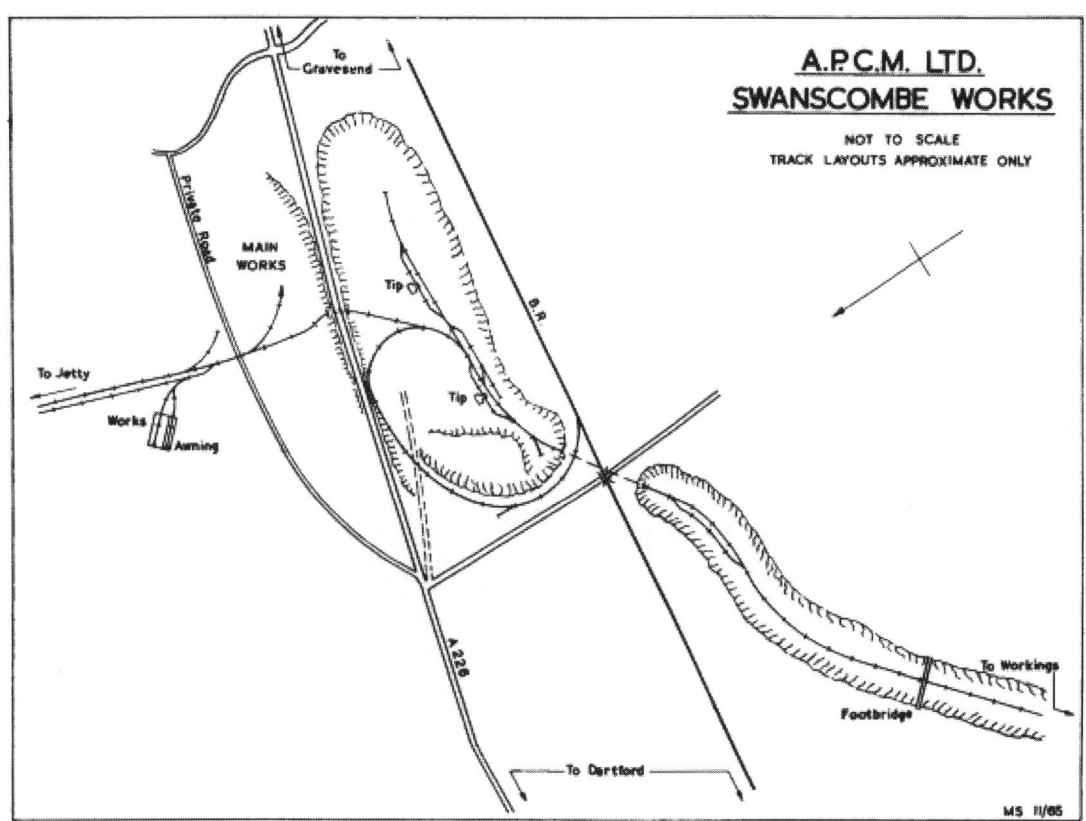

Map of the rail network at A.P.C.M. Swanscombe Works

Locomotive No.4 Approaching Tunnel

Locomotives at the pit 1979 © Tom Burnham

Locomotives at the pit 1979 © Tom Burnham

The Empty Chalk Pit 2011

Swanscombe Works Closure 1990

Article in the Kentish Times 6th September 1990

Cement giant "Blue Circle" is to close its Swanscombe Works with the loss of 180 jobs. The move is part of a package of changes to the borough's industry that will bring 100 job cuts to the firms Northfleet factory. Staff say the decision has come as no surprise, but are shocked at the time-scale of the move. Blue Circle say the closure will take effect from November 30th 1990, and union bosses suspect the company of timing it with the changes at Northfleet. Kevin Stevens, representative of the electricians union the EEP-TU at Swanscombe, says the announcement was taken with an air of resignation. He said "The closure was inevitable given the lack of investment at the site". "Perhaps if we had been able to get the chalk under Darenth Park things would have been different". Derek Warren for the branch at Northfleet, claims in his 20 years with the company he has never known a works closed more quickly. He said, "I believe they are trying to kill two birds with one stone". "When they brought in the re-structuring here in January some people wanted to leave but told they couldn't". "Our retraining is due to begin in November and some of those from Swanscombe can be moved to take their place at Northfleet. Blue Circle's marketing manager Tony Edye agreed there have been problems. He said, "There may be some people at Northfleet who would like to be made redundant but whose skills we need". And he also blamed a lack of chalk supplies for the closure of the London Road plant. The company's chief executive Ian Mckenzie claims it would cost to much modernize. He said, "the decision has been taken in light of the groups policy to ensure all plants remain fully cost effective and competitive". Production of white and sulphate resisting cements, the materials Swanscombe Works specialized in, is being moved to the Danish Blue Circle company we have recently purchased. Mr Edye says the move is part of a company policy to become a pan-European supplier. Ironically, the Swanscombe plant gave up its independent status in 1900 to merge with others in order to beat off foreign competition. Mr Edye added, "No decision has yet been taken as to what will become of the site.

These two pictures show the Works in 1986 and the cement chimneys being demolished January 1993

Eastern Quarry

The two large quarry's one being the current bluewater site and Eastern Quarry supplied chalk to the White Works and Northfleet, and has been closed now for some time. There are two tunnels which connect the two pits.

Eastern Quarry will be transformed into a new residential community with up to 6,250 homes set in a series of "villages".

Homes will benefit from over 20 acres of new parks, lakes and woodland areas and will be connected to Ebbsfleet, Bluewater, Dartford and Gravesend by Fastrack, - a real alternative to the car for local journeys.

Each of the villages' character will be established through careful masterplanning. Design guides will be introduced to ensure a consistent level of high quality and visual identity throughout the development. All residents will have easy access to local shops, parks and community facilities.

At the heart of the development will be the market Centre, with leisure, retail, education and other social and community facilities. The scheme also provides a wealth of employment opportunities with a total of 1.29 million sq ft of office space.

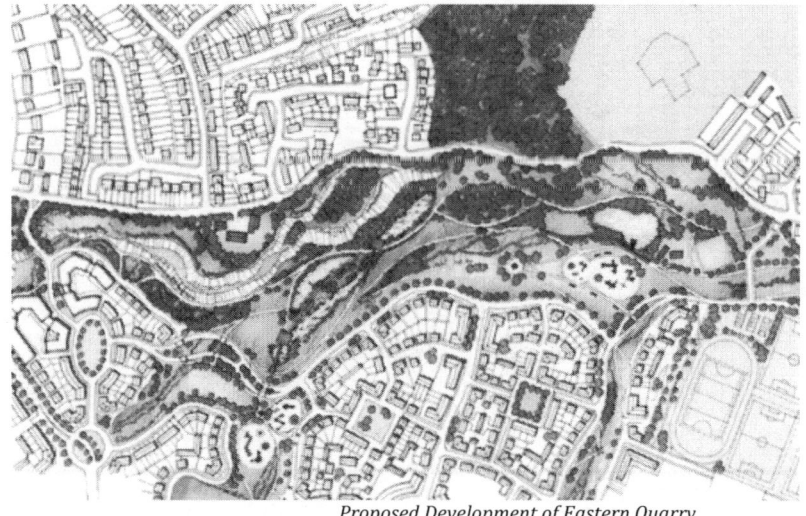

Proposed Development of Eastern Quarry

Chapter 5

**Galley Hill Man
&
Swanscombe Woman**

Galley Hill Man

The fossil remains of the famous Galley Hill man, and associated bones, were found by a workman in, September 1888, when the gravels which cap the terrace were being removed to uncover the underlying chalk for quarrying on the north side of the hill. The then headmaster of the village school, Matthew Hayes was shown the bones protruding from the gravel eight feet below the surface after they had been exposed. School duties prevented Mr Hayes from taking any immediate action himself, and so it happened that an amateur archaeologist, Robert Elliott. On reaching the Galley Hill pit, Mr Elliott found Jack Allsop busily screening gravel and keeping a sharp eye for such things. Jack had something of particular interest for his visitors namely a human skull, which he found in a sandy clay layer. The Skull was eight feet from the surface and two feet above the chalk.

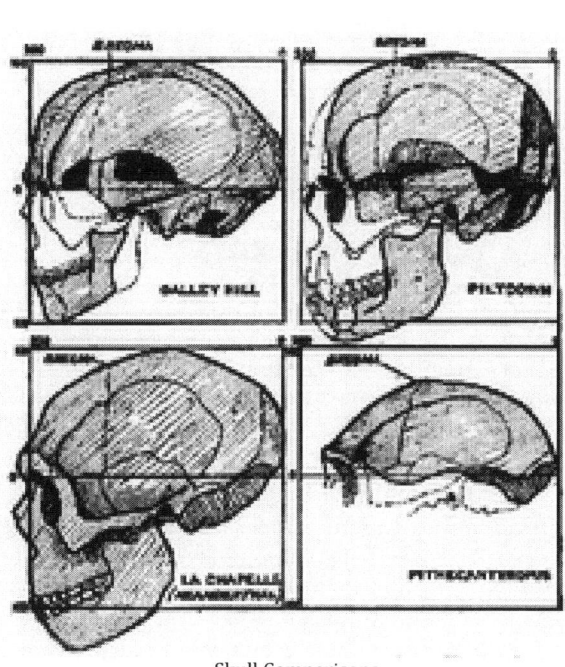
Skull Comparisons

Arthur Keith and Galley Hill Man Bones

Fluorine Test Results 1949

The Galley Hill Skeleton was found 8 feet deep in gravels at Swanscombe, Kent, in 1888. The gravels are Middle Pleistocene, that is to say of early palaeolithic age; and there has been a long controversy as to whether the human bones had been naturally buried in the gravels when they were laid down by the Thames, a quarter of a million years ago, or whether they had been buried artificially at a comparatively recent date. We collected a number of fossil animal bones from these early palaeolithic gravels, a number from later palaeolithic (i.e. Upper Pleistocene) deposits in neighbouring pits, and some from recent deposits, including part of a Saxon skeleton. These were analysed in the Government Laboratory and it was found that all the undoubted early palaeolithic bones contained around 2 per cent. Fluorine, the later palaeolithic around 1 per cent., and those from recent deposits 0.3 per cent. Or less, down to 0.05 per cent. Some spare scraps of the Galley Hill Man had been left in the Museum Collection by one of the original investigators, and we submitted these for analysis. They showed around 0.3 per cent. Fluorine. Yet the skeleton had been found in gravels in which the genuine fossil animal bones show 2 per cent. Fluorine. Clearly the skeleton is not a quarter of a million years old as has been alleged, but is a comparatively recent burial, almost certainly less than 10,000 years old.

Swanscombe Woman

Barnfield Pit, Swanscombe, is one of the important archaeological sites in the United Kingdom. It is best known as the home of the oldest human fossil in Northwest Europe, (scientific name being "Homo sapian steinheimensis"). Because of the fragments of skull which were found there in 1935, 1936 and 1955.

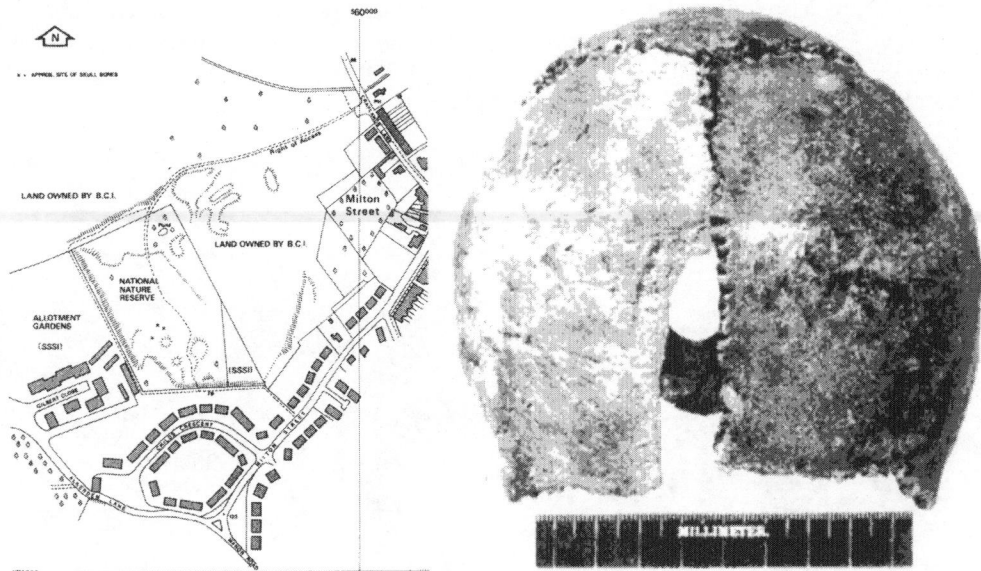

Map showing the location of the Swanscombe Skull and a photograph of the three parts of the Skull shown together.

Tens of thousands of flint implements have also been found there together with the bones of many animals. Lions and elephants were among a wide range of animals, which once roamed the valley. Large collections of flint implements and animal bones were made when the pit was commercially worked for both chalk and gravel.

On Saturday 29th June 1935 Alvan T Marston, a dentist with an interest in the Palaeloithic, was searching the quarried faces in Barnfield Pit for flint tools. In one face, six feet above the pit floor, he spotted what he thought might be a bit of bone sticking out. On closer inspection, as a dentist, immediately recognized it as a human occipital bone, part of the base of the skull at the back. Despite the possibility of subsequent controversy over its position, he realized he couldn't leave it where it was, so marked the spot, left the bone in the keeping of the local chemist, left a note begging the foreman not to dig the site away before more detailed examination and sent an urgent telegram to the British Museum. Nine months later, on Sunday 15th March 1936, having spent most of his weekends searching near the same spot and being bitter and frustrated over the lack of the official support for further investigation, Marston found another part of the same skull, the parietal. The third part was found 20 years later on Saturday 30th July 1955, during investigations by John Wymer at a spot more that 80 feet from the previous discoveries.

Alvan T Marston at Barnfield Pit, 31st July 1955 (From the Wymer Collection)

The Swanscombe Centre

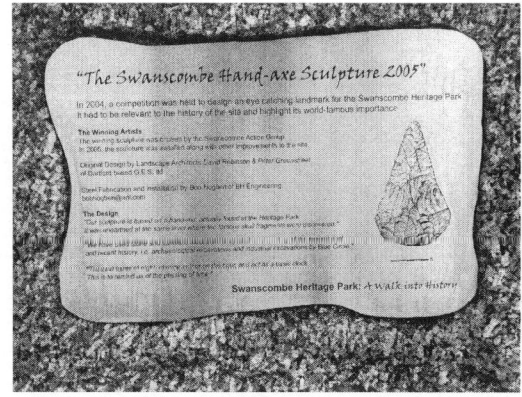

The Swanscombe Centre
was opened by Robert Dunn MP for Dartford
Friday 22nd September 1989

The Skull Site

Site of the first piece of the Skull found in 1935

 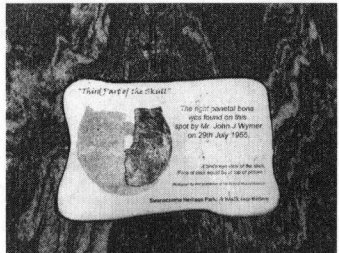 

The Stones showing the locations of the second and third pieces of the Skull 1936 and 1955

Photographs of the 1971 dig site at Barnfield Pit and A T Marston the finder of the first two pieces of the Swanscombe Skull

Chapter 6

Places and Buildings to Remember
Proposed Almshouses 1911
Electric Jubilee Wardona Cinema
Alkerden Farm
Manor House
White's House of Concrete
Mansion House
Swanscombe Recreation Ground 1932
Fire Station & Library
Council Offices
Oast Houses
Swanscombe Swimming Baths

Proposed Almshouse 1911

View of Almshouses (when completed), Milton Street, Swanscombe, Kent

THE

Swanscombe Consolidated Almshouse Charities.

Trustees.

Mr. W. ETHERINGTON   Mr. W.F. STEVENS
Mr. A. JARMAN   Mr. W. TREBBLE

The above illustration shows the building scheme the Trustees have in view for providing Almshouses in Swanscombe, consisting of three separate houses, each providing accommodation for eight aged and infirm persons to live rent free, together with a small weekly contribution to each person from the funds of the Charities.

The Middle house only is just now built, and contains an extra room to be used in common by the alms persons. Each person has the use of a separate room, or a married couple has two rooms with a small scullery, each room is about 12ft by 12ft. in area, and the cost of this house was about £450, defrayed from a long accumulation of the funds of the Charities.

This outlay has practically exhausted these funds, and the Trustees now venture to make an earnest appeal to all these buildings.

The Trustees would be pleased to forward any further information regarding this scheme on enquiry.

LIST OF THE SWANSCOMBE CHARITIES

I. "Daniel's", This is a rent charge of £1 for ever, upon a house and lands called "Daniels's", bequeathed to the poor of this parish by Martin Meriall, in his last will, dated September 8th 1568.

II. "Bear's Almshouses". John Beare, of Swanscombe, died February 29th 1587, and by his will left three Almshouses to this parish. This charity is still in existence and affords accommodation for six alms persons in High Street, Greenhithe.

III. "Anthony Poulter's". This is a rent charge of £1 for ever upon laid situated in Greenhithe, by the will of Anthony Poulter, dated 1635

IV. "Poor's Acre". The earliest record of this century runs this: "December 24th. 1694. Distributed the 20s, due out of Allins to the poor in Swanscombe." It is the recent exchange of this Poor's Acre with the Associated Portland Cement Manufacturers, Limited for the site of the new Almshouses, containing 170ft. frontage, which has enabled the Trustees to formulate their building scheme.

V. "Lady Swan's." This is a bequest of freehold land and buildings for ever, situated in Greenhite Street, consisting of over a quarter of an acre in extent, by Lady Swan in her will made December 4th 1721, for the benefit of the poor in Swanscombe. This is the most important existing charity belonging to the parish.

VI. A legacy of £200 to the Swanscombe Charities form the late Mrs. Head, of Greenhithe, received November 22nd 1898.

The new Almshouse will be opened by Mrs.H.K.G.Bamber on
Wednesday, Januuary 4th 1911, at 2 o'clock

The Almshouse project, which is shown in the above drawing, shows the intention of the Trustees to build a row of Almshouses in Milton Street but due to finances and delays, only the centre section was ever finished. Which comprised of 4 flats. I can only assume that the Great War of 1914-18 must have had an impact on any future planned developments. However the remainder of the land was sold over time, this was no doubt to keep the 4 flats in order.

Up until the 1980's the flats were rent free to the residents, who had to be poor people of the parish 50p weekly benefit was paid to each person. There was only one bathroom in the building, which was shared by all the occupants.

In the late 80's the property was updated, as bathrooms were installed in each flat, as well as central heating whereupon a weekly maintenance charge or rent was applied, with the approval of the Charity Commissioners.

The late Councillor Butcher served as a Trustee for more than 30 years. One of the original Trustees William Stevens name is on a plaque, which is inside the building.

The Electric & Jubilee Cinema 1923-1939

In 1923 the cinema brought the world of films and the images of the age via newsreels to Swanscombe as the Electric Cinema. In 1935 it became the Jubilee Cinema and was owned by local councilor and grocer Mr Charles Mercer, who combined the businesses of entertainment and grocery by having a shack next to the cinema before moving his grocery business to Milton Road. Mercer died in 1943, having lost money on his cinema venture. In typical Swanscombe style the cinema seats were back to front (i.e. the seats faced you at the entrance and the screen was at the front instead of the back of the building). Similarly the expensive seats in Swanscombe were at the front and the cheap seats (with the better view) were at the back. This was so because the sound system was so dreadful only the front seats with the poorer view could hear the film. Nobody could hear the sound when it rained because of the din made on the corrugated iron roof. Children films shown on Saturdays were known as the Saturday Afternoon Crush and the whole cinema was called the 'Bug Hutch' because of its condition. In 1939 it was reconstructed as the Wardona and then closed in 1958. *(From Christoph Bull "Swanscombe in old picture postcards" 2005)*

Jubilee Cinema 1935 and Wardona Court 2011

Wardona Cinema 1939-1958

During the 1910-20's picture houses or nickleodians as they were called were in decline, this was mainly due to the World War 1 and then the depression. At this point in Swanscombe in 1923 at Ames Road, a building with a corregated roof called the Electric Cinema was opened, later renamed the Jubilee. Things did not look good. But there was several embers of hope the acting careers of Ronald Coleman, Victor McLaglen, Leslie Howard and Charles Laughton were starting and although Howard was to be a casualty of WWII these actors along with Balcon and Wilcox were determined that British pictures should survive. Even the son of the Prime Ministers Anthony Asquith joined in to keep the industry alive. But in 1927 Parliament brought in an important piece of legislation the Cinematographers Trade Bill, designed to ensure there was a guaranteed home market for British made films. This meant that 5% of the total number of movies shown in theatres had to be from Britain this figure rose to 20% by 1936. Alfred Hitchcock's Blackmail (1929) is regarded as the first British sound production.

When in 1928 Films with sound were being made, this brought a new dimension to going to the cinema. And so cinemas became to be built almost everywhere. They all had very similar names, such as Majestic, Super, Plaza, Regal and the Wardona. And so in 1935 the Jubilee was demolished and the Wardona was built.

Wardona Cinema in Ames Road c1950

Wardona Openig night 3rd July 1939 by Mrs Jennie Adamson M.P. and Wardona Court in Ames Road 2011

The Wardona, opened its doors for the first time, on Monday July 3rd 1939, by Mrs Jennie Adamson, which was a free event. There were many different acts which were to perform that night.

Opening night poster July 3rd 1935   *The Lady Vanishes Film Poster*

The first film shown that night was The Lady Vanishes strarring Michael Redgrave and Margaret Lockwood, directed by Alfred Hitchcock.

The Wardona was owned and run by Harry Ward to begin with, Mr Hartley took over the cinema. Mr Hartley provided a lot of entertainment for the local community and for Swanscombe Charities. And provided a great distraction to people during the period hardship. Mr Hartley formed a song and dance troupe called "Hartley's Revels" they were a group of girls and boys who sang and danced on the stage, they wore red and gold costumes and sung old time songs such as 'Soldoers of the King' and 'Roses of Picardy' etc. Mr Hartley lived opposite the cinema with Mr & Mrs Skinsley, there son Dick played piano and accordion and played in all the concerts. His daughter Valentine, was killed during a air raid in 1940.

The Wardona was then taken over by Mr Smedley who continued with the entertainment, they were then known as the Swanscombe Revels. They were later bought by Mr Ward.

You entered the cinema through two glass door's, you had a ticket kiosk on your right and large square foyer in the middle. You then went through another two wooden doors where you were met by two usherettes. You then had an isle which went right and left, the toilets were to your right. In front of you was the screen and the stage where the organist came up during intermission in front of this were three blocks of seats isle on the left in the middle and on the right. The usherettes came around and sold drinks and ice cream. The ticket prices were 9d for the front and 1s 10d at the back. My father recalls that often you came out feeling worse than you went in, this was due the fleas which would bite you on the back.

The cinema closed down in the 70's and was used as a warehouse, the building then stood empty and was finally demolished in the 80's. then in 1988 the site became a sheltered housing scheme and was named Wardona Court. And officially opened by Robert Dunn MP in September 1988.

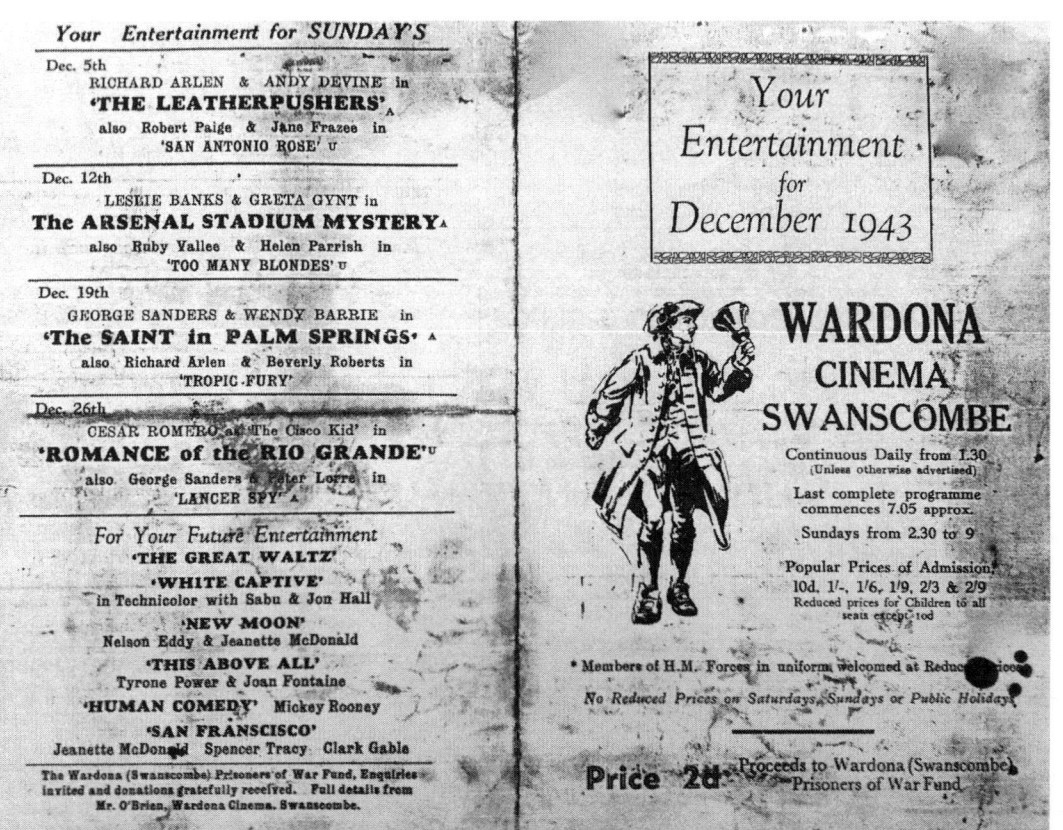

Wardona Cinema Programme of films

Alkerden Farm

The farm dates back to at least 1680, the original farmhouse is still here today with original beams and fireside oven. It's now a barn, but the original walls of lathe and wattle can be still seen in places. Due to large amounts of chalk in the area the cellar was constructed of chalk blocks.

Alkerden Farm c1900   *Alkerden Farm 2011*

The farm today is mostly arable, with 100 acres of grassland. Previously the farm was a large fruit growing area, owned by Mr Chambers but run and managed by Mr Cherry.

In 1958 the orchard was destroyed by a storm of torrential rain and flooding. And subsecquence flooding caused more damage to the fruit trees.

Manor House

The Manor House

Manor Farmhouse, Swanscombe Street. This beautiful building probably began life as the Manor Farm rather than the Manor House, which was possibly situated at the nearby Mansion House. The Child family, who were bankers in London, owned the property from 1740 and probably created what is seen here – as the older building was encased in fashionable eighteenth century brick. In 1872 Thomas Bevan, one of the leading cement manufacturers, purchased this house, along with a vast area of Swanscombe. Over the next century more of the land was progressively turned over to chalk and clay extraction while the farm itself was tenanted out: John Coveney (1866-1880), Robert Stewart (1880-c1896). John and Jack Gunn (1890s to 1950s) and the Pallant family until the early 1960s. The Gunns were local councillors running a jam factory for their fruit (until it was burned down in the 1920s), haulage as well as farming and taking a prominent role in Swanscombe life. Jack Gunn died in 1974 aged 89. Swanscombe Urban District Council bought the house and grounds in the late 1950s and demolished Manor Farm in 1963 replacing it with modern but tasteless council offices, which were themselves demolished in 1989. ((From Christoph Bull "Swanscombe in old picture postcards" 2005)

The Council offices which were built on the site where the Manor House Once stood
And view of the new homes built in 1992 and the entrance to the old offices where you can still make out the words
Swanscombe Urban District Council

Rear of Manor Farmhouse, Swanscombe Street. The view shows the odd building pattern where successive rebuilding had greatly added to any surviving structure from medieval times. Manor Farm and the Mansion House nearby formed part of the Swanscombe Manor Estate until the nineteenth century and as such manorial courts were held here including, possibly, the accusation in 1652 that three Swanscombe women were witches. The Weldon family lived in the manor since the 1570s when Sir Ralph Weldon inherited the manor; both he and his wife Elizabeth have the magnificent alabaster tomb in Swanscombe Church. The Weldons had rented the manor since the 1530s prior to living in Swanscombe. The great parliamentarian leader of Kent during the Civil War (1642-1649) was Sir Anthony Weldon (1583-1648) and it was Sir Anthony who in 1613 obtained Rochester Castle and stripped it of its roof and flooring creating the ruin we see today. It was Sir Anthony who abolished Christmas in 1647 which helped cause an uprising in 1648 and it was Sir Anthony who was determined to await the royalist attack on his manor house and to die fighting – in the event he died peacefully later that year. *(From Christoph Bull "Swanscombe in old picture postcards" 2005)*

View of the same site today 2011

SWANSCOMBE & NORTHFLEET, KENT.

PARTICULARS

OF A VERY DESIRABLE AND VALUABLE

FREEHOLD PROPERTY,

(LAND-TAX REDEEMED,)

KNOWN AS THE

Swanscombe Manor Estate,

Situate in the Parishes of SWANSCOMBE and NORTHFLEET, close to the NORTHFLEET STATION on the NORTH KENT RAILWAY; comprising an old-fashioned Red Brick

MANOR HOUSE,

Well adapted as a Residence for the owner of the Estate, it is situate close to the Church, and approached by a Carriage Drive from the Village, from which it is well screened. Adjoining, are the Stable and Coach-house Premises, and a substantially built

HOMESTEAD,

With Three Hop Oasts and all necessary Farm Buildings; also a detached set of Farm Buildings and Five Cottages; likewise a Valuable Watercress Bed, near Springhead. To the south of the Manor House is a charming Wood of about **150 Acres**, known as

"SWANSCOMBE PARK,"

Commanding extensive views, and offering choice sites for Building. The Arable Land is well adapted for the production of Cereal Crops, Fruit, Hops, and Market Garden produce. There are also about **53 Acres** of Saltings situate on Frackness Marsh. Adjoining to the High Road and near to the Railway there is an exceedingly

VALUABLE CHALK QUARRY AND CLAY DEPOSIT,

Which can readily be utilized for manufacturing into Cement. There is also a Right of Way through Pine Hop leading to the River Thames.

The entire Estate, including the Saltings, comprises an area of about

718 ACRES.

the greater portion of which lies in a ring fence; it possesses some historical interest, and forms an attractive Property for Investment and future occupation.

TO BE SOLD BY AUCTION,

BY

MESSRS. DRIVER,

AT THE MART, TOKENHOUSE YARD, LOTHBURY, LONDON,

On TUESDAY, OCTOBER the 29th, 1872,

At TWO O'CLOCK precisely.

Property will be first offered as an Entirety, the object being to realize as a whole, but if no sufficient bidding as an Entirety, then at the same time and place the Property will be offered in the Two Lots set forth in the following Particulars.

Particulars, with Plan, may be had at the Falcon and Clarence Hotels, Gravesend; the Royal Ship Hotel, Southend; the Bull Hotel, Dartford; the Bell Hotel, Maidstone; the Bull Hotel, Rochester; at the Auction Mart and Estate Exchange, Lothbury, London; of

ALEXANDER BALDERSTON, Esq., Solicitor, No. 32, Bedford Row, London; of
Messrs. R. LAMBERT & SON, Solicitors, 30, Bedford Row, London; of
Messrs. MURRAY, Land and Mineral Agents, No. 24, New Street, Spring Gardens, London; and of
Messrs. DRIVER, Surveyors, Land Agents, and Auctioneers, 4, Whitehall, London.

House of Concrete

Bazley White had his concrete house built at the entrance to the cement works. The house was one of the very first to be largely constructed of concrete and it resembled a Jacobean/Gothic mixture in its architecture, complete with concrete cavalier statues, gables and oriel windows. It became the offices of **Swanscombe** Urban District Council 1926 – 1964, and was demolished later in the 1960s.

Entrance to Swanscombe Cement Works circa 1924. The view shows the house built by John Bazley White, whose family first became partners in Swanscombe Cement Works in 1833. In about 1838 Bazley White built a house for himself at the entrance to his source of fortune, and in Victorian style he was heavily involved in community projects within Swanscombe. Examples of these projects were the establishing of Galley Hill School, All Saint's Church, Galley Hill and Swanscombe Literary Institute. White's grip on Swanscombe was very firm – he controlled matters with his power as a major employer, a major landowner and used his wealth to support community groups he felt would help his control in Swanscombe. As a Victorian 'Lord of the Manor', White would bully the Parish Council or others over rate payments or similar matters. The area shown here was known as 'Swanscombe Cross' – the cross being the meeting of London Road, Craylands Lane and the Cement Works entrance. From 1902 until 1929 this area was the terminus of the Gravesend Tramways system, which brought workers to the gates of the Cement Works, before returning up Galley Hill back to Northfleet and Gravesend. *(From Christoph Bull "Swanscombe in old picture postcards" 2005)*

Same view of the site 2011

John Bazley White's House, Swanscombe Cross. Undoubtedly the most important private dwelling in Swanscombe associated with the cement industry. The house stood at the entrance to the Cement Works – the right of this building was London Road leading to Galley Hill, while the left led straight into the works. John Bazley White had this strange mixture of architectural styles built in the early Victorian years and it was believed to be one of the earliest buildings made from concrete. The Whites moved out and the exterior modified later in the nineteenth century. In September 1926 the building was leased by the Associated Portland Cement Manufacturers (the organization founded in 1900 uniting many independent cement factories) to the newly created Swanscombe Urban District Council- it was known as 'No. 1 Factory House' – neither imagination nor historical accuracy were ever great traits of the cement industry! Swanscombe Council was paying APCM a rent or, £100 per month plus, £13 for an additional room in 1944. Swanscombe Urban District Council vacated the house in 1964 and subsequently this important building was demolished and replaced with waste ground. *(*From Christoph Bull "Swanscombe in old picture postcards" 2005)

Another view taken in 1900

Mansion House

The "Mansion House" c1900

The Mansion House (not to be confused with the nearby Manor House) stood on the south side of Swanscombe Street almost opposite the junction with Church Road. It was believed to have been Elizabethan (1558-1603) but as this picture shows it was massively altered in the nineteenth century During the mid- to late-nineteenth century it was occupied by various families, including the Russells, who also lived at the Manor House. John Russell was the owner of a large brewery in Gravesend and was twice mayor of that town (1876-1877 and 1898-1899). The most famous occupant was Henry Stopes and his family – especially his daughter Marie Stopes (1880-1958), the pioneer of promoting birth control in the early twentieth century. Henry Stopes rented the house for holidays in Swanscombe looking for prehistoric fossils – he was buried at Swanscombe Cemetery in 1902. The Mansion House and its estate were put up for sale in April 1890 consisting of nearly 29 acres including building land, cottages and shops dotted over Swanscombe. The Mansion House itself consisted of three floors with dining, morning, drawing rooms, six bedrooms, a library with panelled walls, two staircases, a huge kitchen, stabling and a gardener's cottage. The house was subsequently rented out, reduced in size before being demolished after 1922. *(*From Christoph Bull "Swanscombe in old picture postcards" 2005)

The driveway in front of the House had a long holly hedge. A man came from the village each year and trimmed and cut it. He would collect and gather the holly, then would make it into wreaths and sell them for use at Christmas. At the top end of the driveway was a large bay leaf tree.

The last family to live in the Mansion House, were Mr & Mrs Hartrup. They used a small house near the morning star pub, to make fish & chips.

Swanscombe Recreation Ground 1932

As more land was acquired for housing so the council decided to create an open space in the shape of **Swanscombe** Recreation Ground. The "movement for a better and brighter **Swanscombe**", which was the council's theme during the 1920s and 1930s, was greatly enhanced by the official opening of the Recreation Ground on 30 April 1932. The complex included:
- A formal park
- bandstand
- Football ground
- bowling green
- Tennis courts
- boating pond
- Public lavatories.

In addition, a drinking fountain was unveiled in memory of Councillor E Moore by his widow.

Swanscombe Recreation Ground 1932 (Taken by Len Todd)

Swanscombe Recreation Ground 1932. The opening of the new Recreation Ground on 30 April 1932 was one of 'Swanscombe's great days of civic history. Swanscombe Urban District Council, using locally produced materials and local unemployed men to create this magnificent new facility. And had relieved the appalling high rate of unemployment. The opening day was a Saturday with warm sunshine and was attended by crowds of local people in addition to civic dignitaries from Swanscombe, Northfleet, Gravesend and Stone. The ground was officially opened by Councillor, Alexander Entwhistle, the chairman of the council for 1930-1931 amid a huge sense of local pride and achievement. This view shows the new bandstand, the hop kilns and oast houses in the background (now used as an old people's welfare and social centre) and the boundary between the park and the cemetery. In an age of simple pleasures 'Rose Sunday' attracted crowds to the park and cemetery to see the exceptional displays of Swanscombe roses. *(*From Christoph Bull "Swanscombe in old picture postcards" 2005)

The Official Opening 1932 (Taken by Len Todd)

Swanscombe Councillors, 1932. The proud civic day of the official opening of Swanscombe's Recreation Ground on 30th April 1932 is shown here with the local councillors and officials gathered on the bandstand. The three councillors at the front are: (left) William Everard of Everards, the shipping company in Greenhithe, who was chairrnan of the Unemployment Grants Scheme Committee. In the centre is Thomas Broad, chairman of Swanscombe Urban District Council 1932-33 and chairman of the Works Committee. On the right is Alexander Entwhistle, chairman of the Urban District Council 1930-1932 who is accepting the silver key to officially open the Recreation Ground. Other councillors present on this occasion were John Gunn (of Manor Farm), Walter Ames, William Knight, Thomas Wedgewood Ostle, Thomas Tutt, Arthur Allen, Thomas Bodle, Albert Frost, Arthur Lane, Thomas Coveney, Stanley Fright, Peter Fletcher and R.W Butcher. (From Christoph Bull "Swanscombe in old picture postcards" 2005)

Swanscombe Fire Brigade putting on a show 1932 (Taken by Len Todd)

Water Fountain 1932 (Taken by Len Todd)

Memorial Fountain, Recreation Ground, Swanscombe, 1932. The fountain is part of the facilities of the Recreation Ground, dedicated to the memory of Councillor Edward Moore, who died in 1932. Moore was part of a political dynasty whose financial security was originally in the Moore Brothers Mineral Water Company of 59 Milton Road, Swanscombe, Edward Moore lived in Dartford but represented Galley Hill Ward on Swanscombe Urban District Council. Moore was a very keen councillor in the creation of a 'Better and Brighter Swanscombe' campaign during the 1920s and 1930s, of which the Recreation Ground formed part. Another member of the Moore Family was George Moore, who was chairman of Swanscombe's council in 1936-1937. The fountain provided water for humans at the top and at the bottom was another watering area for dogs. Today the fountain exists but no longer provides water. . *(From Christoph Bull "Swanscombe in old picture postcards" 2005)*

The Boating Pond 1932 (Taken by Len Todd)

Boating Pond, Recreation Ground, Swanscombe, 1932. A major feature of Swanscombe's new Recreation Ground was the boating pond which, despite many local children falling in, was visited by people from miles around the area. The pond was greatly used by model boat enthusiasts and in the 1930s saw many 'pop-pop' boats on it. These were powered by a candle, which heated a tiny boiler in the vessel, thus creating steam and this caused the popping noise as the boats went across the water. Sailing boats, barges, clockwork boats were all seen on the pond. Elderly residents' model sailing boats that floated off had to be rescued by the local youth who waded into the pond with rolled-up trousers to retrieve the vessels. During the Second World War, by which time the pond was already leaking, this facility was used for roller-skating and cycles – having been drained of water first! The railings behind mark where Park Road was about to be built and in the background can be seen Swanscombe Woods on its hilly position, a place beloved by Swanscombe folk for picnics. . *(From Christoph Bull "Swanscombe in old picture postcards" 2005)*

Swanscombe Recreation Ground 2011

Swanscombe Recreation Ground 2011

Water Fountain 2011

Swanscombe Fire Service

Swanscombe Firemen 1900

Swanscombe Fire Station Church Road 1908

Swanscombe Fire and Police Service 1900

Swanscombe Parade c1924

It was with great civic pride that the fire station in Church Road was officially opened on Saturday, 13th June 1908. Swanscombe Parish Council had been very keen to establish a properly organized fire service in the 1890's and by 1898 – 1899 a temporary fire station had been established at Galley Hill (in addition to one at Greenhithe). In 1907 land at the south end of the Primitive Methodist Chapel was for sale and purchased by Swanscombe Parish Council. In Novemeber 1907 plans were drawn up for a new fire station and proposals for a first floor council chamber were dropped, to be taken up again in the 1920's. The opening day saw a parade of neighbouring fire brigades. The fire engines were led by Swanscombe's Captain A.E.Kent (1872-1940) and preceded by the band of the training ship 'Arethusa'. The church bells were ringing, flags out and a huge crowd assembled in the streets. . (From Christoph Bull "Swanscombe in old picture postcards" 2005)

Swanscombe Urban District Dennis Fire Engine c1929

The Old Fire Station, which had the library on the first floor c1949

The building shown above still remains in Church Road. Swanscombe Urban District Council operated the fire brigade until 1941, when the National Fire Service was set up in response to the Second World War. In 1948 Kent County Council became responsible for the county's fire brigade services, the vehicle seen here is a modified Bedford lorry, which was a utility fire engine created at the beginning of the Second World War. Swanscombe Branch Library occupied the upper floor of the building from 1928 until moving down to the ground floor in 1968. The upper floor was added to the single storey fire station 1922 as a council chamber but vacated by Swanscombe Council in 1926. The entrance to the library was along the alleyway on the left side of the building and then via a back door and flight of wooden stairs. *(From Christoph Bull "Swanscombe in old picture postcards" 2005)*

Swanscombe Fire engine at the recreation ground, 1932. The vehicle shown here and on the previous page is the purpose built Dennis fire engine, which replaced the previous Garfield converted motorized lorry as the urban's district's main fire fighting appliance in 1929. Captain Albert Ernest Kent is fourth from the left in the front row. Kent retired from fire fighting in 1929 after a stroke, but remained as chief for ceremonial occasions after this. Next to captain Kent can be seen Burt Ellen, with a huge goiter on the side of his face.

Swanscombe Fire Service

Swanscombe Parish Council.

GALLEY HILL, SWANSCOMBE, KENT,

M. H. HEYS, CLERK.

Feby 6th 1900.

A List of Captains and Members of Fire Brigade as prepared by the Fire Brigade Committee for the approval of the Council Meeting to be held Feby 6th.

Geo Wolfe — Captain	Florence Cotts, Swanscombe
Arthur Lane	Knockhall Chase, Greenhithe
Wm Turrell	2 " Cottages — do —
Ar Joel	Knockhall do
F A Miller	Station Road do
J E Hayward	2 Provident Street do
Ern't Scutts	1 Hope Villas, Knockhall Chase
Geo Poll	15 Francis Cotts, Swanscombe
G A Bardoe	Broomfield Road do
F Moore	4 Selina Cotts do
A Bain	Castle Street do
H G Head	Galley Hill
I Warwood	Castle Street

The above is the Council's proposed list for the appointment of the Firemen in Swanscombe 1900

Swanscombe Fire Service Continued

OVER FORTY YEARS A FIREMAN

Mr. A. E. Kent, Of Swanscombe

Mr. ALBERT ERNEST KENT, 67, 92, Milton Road, Swanscombe, for well over 40 years a fireman in Kent and Surrey, died on Sunday.

He was honorary chief of Swanscombe Fire Brigade for more than ten years, receiving the honour when he retired through ill-health.

Before that he was for 25 years captain of the Brigade and a fireman for five. He served for several years in Weybridge and Walton-on-Thames Brigade before he came to Kent.

Mr. Kent possessed a large collection of medals and trophies which he was awarded.

He received a medal for saving a fireman from a burning house, and won the coveted Blenheim Palace medal. He took part in hundreds of tournaments and wore a medal for his 30 years' service in Swanscombe.

Two sons and five daughters are left, in addition to the widow.

The funeral will be at Swanscombe on Saturday. The coffin will be borne on Swanscombe Fire Engine. Firemen from many other brigades will probably attend.

LATE MR. A. E. KENT.

Swanscombe Fire Service 2011

Swanscombe Fire Station 2011 (front an back)

Swanscombe Dennis Sabre Fire Engine

Swanscombe Firemen 2011 (left to right)

Edward Brine 'Firefighter', Shaun Hooper 'Firefighter', John Allwright 'Watch Manager', Ian Gillingham 'Firefighter'
Alan Reach 'Firefighter', John Hooper 'Firefighter', Keith Wellard 'Firefighter'

Swanscombe Library 1928 – 1998
The Story of a Public Library Pioneer
By Christoph Bull. B.A. (Hons), A.L.A.

The joy and pride of Swanscombe providing free reading for its citizens in the 1920s is perhaps hard for us today to comprehend – it would be something akin to providing each citizen with a free computer, free internet connection and an I-Reader all wrapped in one – a fantastically forward looking idea for the citizens of a small industrial town like Swanscombe. One must always remember that for most Swanscombe citizens there was very little money to spend on luxuries like books after food and rent had been paid – and even more difficult if there were family problems such as debt, gambling or drinking – Swanscombe Urban District Council knew that education and decent recreation were two methods for families unable to afford to buy books or go to Gravesend to use the library to try and break out into a great new world to find escape and improvement for their often harsh lives.

Having built and paid for the very first building to be owned by the council (the Fire Station in 1908), the council wanted to now use the room above the fire station (added in 1922) for the benefit of all citizens. Swanscombe Urban District Council knew they were too small to provide a library service on their own (unlike both Gravesend and Dartford who did run their own independent services), so it was decided to join forces with the newly created Kent County Council's Public Libraries service, known as Kent County Library. Kent Council Library offered library services to all towns and villages that did not already run their own – and the more help these smaller places gave to the County Library, the better the service provided. Swanscombe offered the room above the Fire Station as accommodation and after the meetings with Miss A S Cooke (Kent's First County Librarian 1921-1943) the service began in November 1928 – at first with a volunteer, but by 1929 Swanscombe was one of the very first pioneer Kent County Library branches with paid staff – even by 1933 there were only four of these in Kent – and two of those (Swanscombe and Greenhithe) were within Swanscombe Urban District. In 1968 the library moved from the room above the Fire Station to the ground floor after the fire station moved to its new location – and continued until 2002 when it was transferred to Swan Valley School. In 2010 it was moved to the ground floor of the school building and shares a space with a café making for a relaxed atmosphere and offering all the services needed such as books, local history and computers.

Swanscombe Library 1998
Photo Courtesy of Moira Griffiths

Old Fire Station Café 2011

Council Offices

Official Opening by T.Bodle 26th September 1964

Notes from the Official Opening Programme

There are three parts to the new council offices: a two storey building containing Clerk's and the Surveyor's Offices, the council chamber, and the committee room. These three parts are arranged so that they enclose an outdoor court and entrance hall. There is a paved terrace on the roofs of the entrance hall and committee room with access from the first floor of the office building.

Smooth charcoal grey bricks, aluminum, western red cedar and glass have been used externally throughout and these will reduce maintenance costs to the minimum. The structure is load bearing brickwork, ground floor and first floor of the office building are concrete, and all roofs are timber covered with ashphalte.

The brickwork of the two-storey office building has been constructed to form U-shaped piers. These piers are 4ft apart. On the outside walls aluminum frames filled with obscured or clear glass run up the full height of the buildings, on the inside walls framing the corridors there are timber frames with doors and glazed panels. Cupboards are built into the U-shaped piers for every office.

The roof of the council chamber is constructed of built up timber trough beams with plastic roof lights spanning between them and fluorescent tubes for artificial light recessed into the bottom of each trough. The form of this roof has been designed to give good lighting and good characteristics to the chamber.

The internal ceilings and walls are plastered; various floor finishes have been used including terrazzo for the staircase. Apart from the cupboard doors which are painted, all internal woodwork is left natural with a sealer applied to prevent it getting dirty.

The building is centrally heated by gas fired furnaces. These furnaces provide warm air which is blown through ducts low level outlet grills placed in every room. Temperature is thermostatically controlled and local adjustments can be made by manually adjusting the grilles. The system is zoned so that the supply of heat to different parts of the building can be cut off when not is use. This kind of heating and that regulated supply of fresh air, cleaned and humidified, is provided.

The grounds surrounding the building have been landscaped in consultation with the KCC Estates Department; new furniture and furnishings have been obtained through the KCC supplies department, and ancillary building such as the entrance gates, garages, and garden shelter have been built with the same materials, and similar detailing to those used for the council offices themselves.

The contract has been carried out by the councils own labour force under the control of the Surveyor and the supervision of the of the buildings superintendent. A high standard of workmanship has been maintained throughout the work.

Swanscombe Urban District Council 1926-1974

On The 9th April 1926 the first Chairman of the newly formed District council was appointed his name was Walter Ames, he was the first of many chairman over the years ending with Patrick Gerard Melvin in 1973-74.

1926-27	Walter Ames	1950-51	Thomas Bodle
1927-28	Rev Stanley J W Morgan	1951-52	William Owen Keary
1928-29	Edward Moore Snr	1952-53	Mrs Maggie Jane Wright
1929-30	Frank Lund	1953-54	Howard Eric Durrant
1930-31	Alexander Entwistle	1954-55	Charles William Butcher
1931-32	Alexander Entwistle	1955-56	Alfred Frederick Siggers
1932-33	Thomas G H Broad	1956-57	Thomas Bodle
1933-34	John Edwin Gunn	1957-58	Peter Connolly
1934-35	William Joseph Everard	1958-59	Leonard Thomas Owen
1935-36	William Joseph Everard	1959-60	Frederick Harry John Garland
1936-37	George Moore	1960-61	Gilbert Charles Hammond
1937-38	Arthur William Lane	1961-62	Mrs Maggie Jane Wright
1938-39	Peter Fletcher	1962-63	William Owen Keary
1939-40	Thomas Bodle	1963-64	Charles William Butcher
1940-41	Edwin Hills	1964-65	Thomas Bodle
1941-42	William James Webb	1965-66	Leonard Thomas Owen
1942-43	William Alfred Knight	1966-67	Peter Connolly
1943-44	Arthur Sydney Knight	1967-68	Gilbert Charles Hammond
1944-45	Rev Stanley J W Morgan	1968-69	Mrs Maggie Jane Wright
1945-46	Rev Stanley J W Morgan	1969-70	William Owen Keary
1946-47	Rev Stanley J W Morgan	1970-71	Charles William Butcher
1947-48	Rev Stanley J W Morgan	1971-72	Anthony James Rayfield
1948-49	Dewi Taylor Williams	1972-73	Stanley Hearn
1949-50	Walter Austen	1973-74	Patrick Gerard Melvin

Walter Ames   George Moore   Edward Moore Snr

Article in the Reporter 14th August 1964

The site of what is perhaps the oldest farm in Swasncombe, it was mentioned in the Domesday Book has become the site of Swanscombe's brand new £35,000 Council Offices. The council staff moved in on Tuesday of last week. The memory of Manor Farm in Manor Road, has however been kept alive by the preservation of the 100 year old oast house to be used as a store. A number of old trees have also been preserved. To give the new offices an arboreal setting which contrasts sharply with the gloomy 130 year old buildings which the council had inhabited since 1926 in London Road. Once space in the new building is twice that of the old building, and £4,000 has been spent on furnishings and floor coverings. Only the best of the councils old equipment has been kept. There is now a staff restroom and kitchen, Mr Frederick Stuart, Clerk of the council, said that he felt sure the improved surroundings would induce better work all-round. Until it bought the Manor Farm in 1958, Swansombe council had been dogged with bad luck over the purchase of new sites. The first one bought was needed for housing after the Second World War, and the second had to be written off as unsuitable. The remainder of the three-acre Manor Farm site is to be converted into a children's playground and park.

Swanscombe Urban District Council Dust Cart, c1939. A great symbol of municipal pride was the dustcart emblazoned in the council's livery. The above was registered in 1939 and was a dustless loader, petrol-driven freighter manufactured by Shelvoke & Drury. Rubbish was collected from the rear of properties via the network of alleyways and then loaded into the carts, which had a terrific choice of pits in which to dump Swanscombe and Greenhithe's refuse. The main pit was a disused chalk quarry at the rear of Barnfield Pit, off Craylands lane. Swanscombe Urban District Council's refuse service is remembered for its efficiency and the council had already been using motor vehicles since 1930 when an Eagle-Thornycroft refuse cart was purchased to modernize the horse drawn fleet. . (From Christoph Bull "Swanscombe in old picture postcards" 2005)

New Offices

New Council Offices built in 2006

Article in the Dartford Messenger 2nd February 2006

A Dream is becoming a reality for members of a town council after years of waiting for their own offices. The diggers are due to move on the site on Monday to turn the soil of what will become Swanscombe & Greenhithe Town Council's own purpose built new home. With a price tag of £1.3m the two storey building has not come cheap. However, councilors insist the building is necessary if they are to cope with a huge scale of regeneration over the next decade. The office will be constructed on land at the Milton Road playing fields, off the Grove in Swanscombe.

Oast Houses

Oast Houses c1920

An Oast House is a building used to dry fresh hops before they are sent to the brewers, to be used for flavouring beer. Beer was not produced within the oast house itself, but some malthouses (breweries) did incorporate drying kilns for drying barley for malt.
The *oast* was a kiln, with a plenum chamber fired by charcoal at ground floor and the drying floor directly above. The steep pitched roof 105hanneled the hot air through the hops to the top. A cowl on the top of the roof allowed the hot air ('reek') to be drawn up through the kiln in a vacuum effect. The cowl pivoted to control the air extraction and stop rain getting in.
The *stowage*, was the barn section, it had a cooling floor and press at first floor and storage area at ground floor. The dried hops were taken from the drying floor to cool and be packed using a hop press. The press packed hops in a large sack called a 'pocket' suspended to the ground floor where the pockets were stored to await collection.

Oast Houses c1910

Remains of the Oast Houses 2011

Swanscombe Swimming Baths

Swasncombe Baths c1950

At the bottom of Knockhall Road at the London Road end, you will pass the Greenhithe sign. On the corner you will see some flats and beyond that houses. And in 1982 you would have seen fences which surrounded a council depot. But before 1982 you would have seen Swanccombe Urban District Councils bold attempts to bring modern living to an already heavily industrialized area. Even beating both Dartford and Gravesend with its up to date amenities . In 1935 the foundations were laid. Then on the 8th August 1936 with a cost of £5,800 and a grand opening event Swanscombe baths opened its doors for the first time. To get in, the entrance was over the road off Flint Cottages, you were then greeted by the ticket office. Then you saw the swimming pool and for many would have been their first sight of clear blue water. The kiosk at the east end of the pool sold refreshments and conveniences for visitors when on those really hot days always sold well. The pool was 120 feet by 60 feet, it has a up-to-date purification plant and the water was heated by oil fuel. At on end were the dressing cubicles, showers and foot baths. In later years a diving board was installed as per the picture above. Its decline happened in the 1970's when neighbouring towns started to provide modern indoor pools. So it was with sadness from the local area that the Swimming Pool was closed in 1982, and thus was lost yet another memorable landmark from the area. I do remember myself going swimming there with my dad and brother and later when it was vacant and being made ready to be demolished.

Laying the foundations in 1935 and Swimmers enjoying the opening and Official opening 8th August 1936 Courtesy of Tips Images

Swimming Baths c1930

Site of the old Swimming Baths now Flats and Houses. And Flint Cottage

This site at London Road was once a busy one now long since gone were a gatehouse with a building for coaches and horses to stay for the night with lodgings for the drivers.

Old entrance gate to the Mortuary now disused houses

If you have walked down London Road and looked at this old gate and wondered what it was, well it was the entrance to the old mortuary, which was above the wall. You went through the gate up the steps and went in the front of the building around the back opposite Flint Cottage is where the bodies were brought.

The site now is disused houses and land. Which was bought by, the old managers of Blue Circle so they could overlook the entrance to the cement works and I suppose not have to far to got to work.

Chapter 7

Transport Trams and Trains

Transport Trams & Trains

Transport facilities to growing **Swanscombe** improved on 22 September 1902, when the newly constructed electric tramway, from Denton **through** Gravesend and Northfleet reached the parish. The trams ran along the London Road with stops at the George and Dragon on Galley Hill and Craylands Lane, where the trams turned around and returned eastwards. The tram conductors shouted "Holy City" when stopping at **Swanscombe**. This curious name was linked to the fact that **Swanscombe** was surrounded by pits or holes and "Holy" was really "Holey". The terminus at Craylands Lane (**Swanscombe** Cross) was only 1½ miles from that of Dartford's trams at Horns Cross. The South Eastern and Chatham Railway stopped any attempt at linking the two tram systems, as this would have rivalled their monopoly. In order to placate local opinion, the Railway Company opened a railway halt at Craylands Lane in 1908. The halt's position was on the edge of **Swanscombe** and not well used until moved to its present position in 1930. *(From Christoph Bull "Swanscombe in old picture postcards" 2005)*

Swanscombe Halt 1910 in Craylands Lane

Tram at the top of Galley Hill c1920 and Tram at Northfleet c1920

Swanscombe Halt

By David Glasspool Kent Rail.org

This was one of a number of later wooden platform halts opened by the SE&CR after 1900. "Swanscombe Halt" came into use concurrent with nearby "Stone Crossing Halt" on 2nd November 1908. They both generally served those communities built up around the paper mills and extensive Portland Cement works, which occupied the south bank of the Thames from Stone through to Northfleet. Existing services along the line generally did not stop at these halts; instead, a "railmotor" service was inaugurated, this being a steam locomotive and single carriage sharing a common underframe. These services were run in competition with the expanding tram networks - that tramway from Woolwich ran right through to Dartford, terminating at Horns Cross (Stone). The Gravesend tram network was reached by an eastward trek for approximately a mile, no physical connection between the respective rails ever being made. The halt remained until 1930, when the Southern Railway built a new station from prefabricated concrete (which the company manufactured itself) 840 yards to the east of the original, opening on 6th July of that year. This coincided with the extension of third rail from Dartford and the commencement of electric services to Gravesend. The arrangement at the halt was interesting: rather than the provision of an independent footbridge to link the two platforms, the initiative was instead taken to utilise the adjacent road bridge as a walkway. Flights of steps were carved into the hillsides and as the pictures will reveal, it seems almost like a footbridge was sawn in half and each side used on either platform to complete the descent down from the street. The concept of utilising the high street bridge would naturally be more economical, the company not having to install an additional footbridge. Waiting accommodation here was also generous, a substantial timber shelter being provided on each platform, complete with canopy - these were unlike the SER's clapboard structures, the wooden planks on the former laying flush on the frame, whilst those on the latter overlapped (hence "clapboard" or "weatherboard").

For many years this station remained largely unchanged and unlike its predecessor, it was never built with a refuge siding spurring off the "down" line; this was in light of its, comparatively speaking, remoteness from the cement works. It became just plain "Swanscombe" in May 1969 and was served only by slow trains stopping at all stations - the aforementioned railmotor service had disappeared decades ago, back in the days of the SE&CR. Whereas those shelters at nearby Stone Crossing became concrete, those at Swanscombe remained wooden and over the years fell into a state of disrepair, not helped by vandalism. These 1930-built structures were replaced circa 1995, sadly by much more inferior accommodation - the dreaded bus shelters.

The aforementioned halt is without doubt the least important aspect of Swanscombe's railway history. The first rails came in 1825 when one James Frost opened the country's first cement manufacturing plant in Swanscombe, producing the logically-named "British Cement". Here, a 3ft 5½ inch gauge system appeared, which linked the works adjacent to London Road with the quarries and Thames jetties. For the early years of this railway's existence, horses were used to haul wagons, these of which had a rather unique feature: outside wheel flanges. Interestingly, this system originated from the use of the aforementioned animal haulage, a gap on the outer sides of the rail posing no risk to the hooves of a horse negotiating the track. On new years day 1837, the cement works came under the auspices of John Blazey White & Sons, whom began modernisation of the domestic railway system. This would include the procurement of new motive power in the form of narrow gauge steam locomotives, again with outside wheel flanges for compatibility with the existing track work. The operation was then taken over by the Portland Cement Company in 1900, whom had established a similar factory at Greenhithe in the previous year - by this time, J. B. White & Sons works were producing Keene's Plaster, Frost's Cement and Roman Cement. The Swanscombe cement operation became the most extensive in the North Kent area and in 1928, four 0-4-0 saddle tank locomotives were delivered from Hawthorne Leslie, followed by a fifth the next year, then a sixth in 1935. These deliveries coincided with the conversion from narrow to Standard Gauge, this being completed in its entirety by 1929.

The saddle tanks were reliable and powerful engines, such their success that a sixth of the type arrived in 1948, although its builder was instead the now amalgamated "Robert Stephenson & Hawthorns". Their existence initially came under threat in the early 1960s when a diesel locomotive was experimented on site in view of replacing steam, but it was discovered that it was not suitable for the heavy loads involved, nor for negotiating the appalling track work of the chalk pits. The dawn of the diesels was thus put-off - only for the time being, however. The saddle tanks finally had their swansong in 1971, when diesels assumed command of the pits, but at least four of the engines were saved for preservation. Rail operation in the pits continued until chalk excavation was exhausted in 1982 - a single-line connection with the North Kent Line had been in place since conversion to Standard Gauge in 1929.

Swanscombe Halt c1950

Swanscombe railway station was opend 6th July 1930 and serves the village of Swanscombe in North Kent, England. Train services are operated by Southeastern. The station is awkwardly located in a very deep chalk cutting, with a long staircase from the booking office leading to the up platform. The down platform is reached across a road overbridge and down another long flight of stairs.

The ticket office, on the 'up' side at road level, is located in a recent building. This is manned only during part of the day; at other times a PERTIS passenger-operated ticket machine issues 'Permits to Travel' - which are exchanged on-train or at manned stations for travel tickets - and is located outside the ticket office. Until the 1980s, a separate manned ticket office was located in a building on the eastbound platform.

Swanscombe Station 2011

Chapter 8

Beer & Public Houses

Beer & Public Houses

Dates and Names supplied by **pubhistory.com**

At one time in Swanscombe there were as many as 16 Beer and Pub houses. Some stayed as beer houses, which closed down over time and some stayed and became public houses. The difference between a beer house and pub are, beer houses were allowed to sell ales and beers, whereas public houses are officially licensed premises to sell beers wines and spirits.

Alma, Galley Hill, Swanscombe,

Built in 1860. At Church Road in 1881 census, then by the 1901 census the entry is listed at Alma cottages, and subsequent census entries mention being at the back of the Alma. By 1911, the address is at 26 High Street.

The Alma Public House in 1905 the street sign read Orchard Road, then changed to Alma Road

1881 William Ludlow ,1891 Chas Addison ,1899 Walter Charles Brooker ,1901 Nathan Bobby

1903 Nathan Bobby 1911 Jane Bobby 1913 Mrs Jane Bobby

Badger, Beer House
Galley Hill, Swanscombe, 1733 to 1735
Beer House, not much detail on this place.

Beare, Beer House
Swanscombe, Greenhithe border 1707 to 1742
Beer House, not much detail on this place.

Black Bull, Beer House
Swanscombe, 1742 to 1750
Beer House, not much detail on this place.

Black Eagle, Public House
Galley Hill, Swanscombe 1866 to 1967
1866 - 1967; The Eagle, Botany Bay in 1881 census, then at London Road in 1891, later in Northfleet through boundary changes - demolished in 1968

The Black Eagle was the first building inside Swanscombe Parish. The pub dates from about 1866 and served the Taunton Road community and the expanding industrial areas springing up on the Swanscombe/Northfleet border. As road traffic increased during the 20th century, the corner became dangerous and saw many accidents. It was demolished in 1968 . (From Christoph Bull "Swanscombe in old picture postcards" 2005)

1881 Caroline Taylor 1891 George Elliot 1901 Harry White 1913 Walter Thomas Morgan
1922 Walter Thomas Morgan 1930 Fredk Martin 1938 Geo Stokes

Black Lion, Beer House
Swanscombe, 1715
1715/George Oatley
Beer House, not much detail on this place.

Blue Anchor, Beer House then Public House
Swanscombe, 1735 to Present
1735 to 1965. At Church Road in 1881 census. It was rebuilt in 1965; the Hazel family ran this from the 1890s to 1981

The Blue Anchor Pub (c1905) in Swanscombe where John was living in 1861.The name 'Blue Anchor' is said to have originated in a ancient legend about an anchor and chain just appearing from the sky and a sailor dressed in blue drowning whilst trying to free that anchor. However, I wonder if the name of this pub was taken from the inn of the same name in Somerset, between Minehead and Watchet. George Harper, landlord in 1861 was born East Harptree (near Bath) in Somerset.

The Blue Anchor Pub in 1890 and the official opening in 1965 an the pub in 2011

1840/John Conford 1858/William Harper 1881/William Mae Wiltshire 1891/Charles S Aldred 1901/Robert Hazel 1903/Robert Hazel 1913/William Hazel 1918/William Hazel 1922/William Hazel 1930/William Hazel 1938/William Hazel

Bull, Beer House
Swanscombe, 1707 to 1715
1715/Mary Rossier

Beer House, not much detail on this place.

Coopers Arms, Beer House then Public House
"Bottom House" Craylands Lane Swanscombe, c1840 to c1960
1881/Joseph Holt Wellard 1891/William H Martin 1938/Joseph S Gilbert

George & Dragon, Public House
1 London Road, Galley Hill, Swanscombe, 1843 to 2011
Built in 1843, at Galley Hill Terrace in 1881 census, then at London Road in 1891

George and Dragon taken in 1930 My Grandfather Frederick Durling is 10th from the left back row

Photo taken in 1930 and the Pub sign 2011

George and Dragon Pub now closed and up for sale 2011 and no open again

The George and Dragon was one of Swanscombe's major pubs and was able to provide spirits, accommodation and stabling in addition to beer. It stands on the main Strood to Dartford turnpike road; this section was turnpiked in 1738. The present building is believed to date from the 1840's but an earlier house existed to pick up the passing road trade, until the 1840's Galley Hill was a hamlet physically separate from Swanscombe itself.

1858/William Clinch 1881/John Cottle 1891/Henry Hackman 1901/Thomas Hudson 1913/Thomas Hudson
1938/George H Sparkes

Morning Star, Beer House then Public House

141 Church Road, Swanscombe, 1759 to Currently Closed 2011
1759 - 1940. At Bramfield Road in 1881 census. Destroyed by a bomb in November 1940, when twenty seven people were killed and eleven injured. Rebuilt 1950

Morning Star Pub Bomb Damage 1940 and the Rebuilt Pub as it looks today

Just after 8 o'clock on the evening of Sunday 10 November 1940 a German bomb crashed down directly into The Morning Star Inn, causing in a single explosion, Swanscombe's worst wartime disaster. All that was left after the explosion was, where the pub had stood, a "heap of bricks and twisted rafters" surrounding the smoldering pit that had been the cellar, although the staircase leading to the clubroom upstairs extended up out of the wreckage. Distressed families of those known to be in the pub at the time gathered at the street corners awaiting news of the casualties as bodies were gradually recovered from the ruins.

The official casualty lists revealed the death toll to be 27, with six others seriously injured and five people slightly hurt.

"The landlord was amongst the dead, although his wife and son survived. The barmaid who was killed had given notice the week before the raid but had stayed on that evening because of the match. One of the other victims was a merchant seaman on seven days' leave who had spent two days travelling from Scotland to see his wife and children and was having a drink with his father in the pub at the time of the bombing: both were killed."

My Grandfather Frederick Durling was an ARP warden, and was in the pub on the night of the bombing. He recalls, I was in the pub for a couple of hours watching the Darts which were going on. Then the Air raid warning was sounded. He then drank up his pint said goodbye and left the pub. He then said he got about 200 yards from the pub when he heard the explosion, he turned around and saw the Morning Star pub on fire. He turned around and went to help the injured. He recalls that what he saw was burning bodies and body parts a sight he says which he never forgot.

1881/Benjamin Grant 1891/Edwin Gosling 1891/Edwin Gosling 1901/Richard Martin 1913/John Messam 1930/William Hotson 1938/Mrs Eliz Oram

North Kent Arms, Beer House then Public House
"Middle House" Craylands Lane, Swanscombe, 1900 to 1950

1891/Fanny Selby 1901/John Worwood 1903/John Worwood 1938/Wm J Morris

Prince of Wales, Public House
Galley Hill, Swanscombe, Greenhithe
1893 to 1914; At 4 Prince of Wales Road in 1881 census, then at 5 Edith Cottages in 1891

1881/Ebenezer Brown 1891/Thomas Lovel 1901/Richard Hudson

Rising Sun, Public House
16 Craylands Lane, Swanscombe, 1869 to Present
From 1869. At 1 Milton Terrace in 1881 to 1901 census

The Rising Sun known as the Top House c1890 and the Rising Sun 2011

1881/John Ridgwell 1891/John Ridgwell 1901/John Ridgwell 1930/Mrs Alice Best 1938/Mrs Alice Best

Sun, Public House
16 Swanscombe Street, Swanscombe, 1830 to Present
From 1830; At Church Road in 1881 census. listed in the High Street in 1901 census

1881/Robert Dalton 1891/Herbert A Moss 1901/Charles J Ridgewell 1913/Hy A Tyler 1930/Hy A Tyler 1938/Hy A Tyler

Woodmans Inn, Beer House then Public House
Milton Street, Swanscombe, 1851 to 1920
1851 to 1914; A beer house until 1887
The Woodman was at the end of the walks a place that young couples like to visit, it closed in 1920 but was not pulled down until 1950's

The Woodman c1910

1891/Charles Ridgewell 1901/James Sharpe 1913/James Sharpe

The Wheatsheaf, Beer House then Public House
Galley Hill, Swanscombe, 1860 to Present

Two Photographs of the Wheatsheaf c1920

Chapter 9
A Walk Round Swanscombe
In old and new photographs
And the Good Old Days

Kellys Directory 1899

SWANSCOMBE is a parish, extending to the Thames, three-quarters of a mile from Northfleet station on the North Kent section of the South Eastern railway, 3 west from Gravesend and 4 east from Dartford, in the North Western division of the county, Axton hundred, lathe of Sutton-at-Hone, Dartford petty sessional division, union and county court district, and in the rural deanery of Gravesend and archdeaconry and diocese of Rochester. The church of SS. Peter and Paul is a building, chiefly in the Early English style, and has 6 bells: there are monuments to the Weldons, including those of Anthony Weldon, Eleanor, his wife, and on the south side a monument of alabaster with recumbent effigies of their son, Sir Ralph Weldon kt. ob. 1609, a knight in armour and his lady, both resting their heads on pillows; the nave and aisles were restored by the late Sir James Erasmus Wilson LL.D., F.R.S. who formerly lived here, died in 1884, and was buried in the church; a stained window commemorates the restoration, and there are three others; the church affords 220 sittings. The register dates from the year 1559. The living is a rectory, net yearly value £307, with 39 acres of glebe and residence, in the gift of Sidney Sussex College, Cambridge, and held since 1889 by the Rev. George Hale M.A. of that college. Here are Congregational and Wesleyan chapels, a Primitive Methodist chapel at Galley Hill, a Baptist meeting room at Milton street, and Salvation Army barracks. A burial ground of 5 acres was formed in 1885 at a cost of £493, and is under the control of the Parish Council, but there is no mortuary chapel. Beare's almshouses, founded in 1587 by John Beare, of Greenhithe, for three families, are situated at Greenhithe; the inmates are supported from a charity left in 1721 by Lady Judith Swan, and endowed with half an acre of land, which is let on building and other leases. The income is about £77 a year; each married couple receives 8s. and each single person 5s. 6d. a week. Swanscombe Wood is well known; and here is a cavern called "Clabbernappers Hole."

The extensive cement works of Messrs. John Bazley White and Brothers Lim. at Swanscombe Cross give employment to nearly the whole of the working population here. The Ebbsfleet stream is said to have been formerly navigable. Swanscombe manor house, an ancient building, and the seat of the Weldon family, is now occupied as a farm house. Thomas Bevan esq. D.L., J.P. of Stone Park, near Greenhithe, who is lord of the manor, the trustees of the late Samuel Charles Umfreville esq. of Greenhithe, and Messrs. J. B. White and Bros. Lim. are the principal landowners. The soil is gravel and chalk; subsoil, chalk. The area is 2,137 acres of land, 3 of water, 345 of tidal water and 67 of foreshore; rateable value of the entire parish, £33,885; the population in 1891 was 6,577, including Galley Hill and Greenhithe.

Parish Clerk, Thomas Coombes.

Post, M. O. & T. O., T. M. O., Express Delivery, Parcel Post, S. B. & Annuity & Insurance Office.—Walter Ames, sub-postmaster. Letters received through Greenhithe S.O. delivered at 6.45 & 11 a.m. & 6.15 p.m.; sunday, 6.45 a.m.; dispatched at 7.55 & 10.55 a.m. & 3.10 & 9.10 p.m.; sunday, 10.25 a.m

Galley Hill is an ecclesiastical parish formed from Swanscombe, and will be found under a separate heading.

Knockhall, half a mile west; Western Cross, three-quarters of a mile south-west; Milton street, a quarter of a mile north-west; and Alkerden, half a mile south-west, are hamlets.

National (mixed, boys), erected in 1878, for 250 children; average attendance, 245; Frederick William V. Little, master

National (mixed, girls), erected in 1898, for 144 children; average attendance, 80; Miss Bessie Everett, mist

Infants' erected in 1893 for 200 children; average attendance, 176; Miss Gertrude Chandler, mistress

PRIVATE RESIDENTS.

Brewer Gilbert Devon, Knockhall gro
Cheffins Charles P. E. Riversdale
Dierden William, Athelstan villa
Fuller Thomas, Coomb lodge
Hale Rev. George M.A. Rectory
Hewitt Charles, Knockhall lodge
Homewood Charles S. Knockhall grove
Langston John, Knockhall grove
Ray Walter, Knockhall grove
Reid Alexander M.B
Rodd Richd. 4 Cobham vils. Knockhall
Shrewsbury Rev. George (Congregational), Ingress vale
Styles Mrs. Knockhall
Turrell James, Knockhall grove
Walkling Thos. Mount view, Milton st
Watt Geo. Frederick, Knockhall gro
Wellard Joseph Holt, Fern villa
Wilders Charles, Knockhall grove
Wilders Edward, Knockhall grove

COMMERCIAL

Ainsley Alfred Clarence, shopkeeper
Ames Walter, grocer, draper, clothier, baker, boot & shoe & hardware dealer, Post office
Bartholomew John, farmer
Bobby Elizabeth (Mrs.), confectioner
Carr Georgina (Mrs.), apartments, Knockhall grove
Coombes Brothers, oil & colormen
Coombes Thomas, parish clerk
Coombes Thomas Harry, builder & contractor
Cooper Charles, dairyman
Cooper James North, grocer
Day Charlotte (Mrs.), shopkeeper
Deacon Walter, coal dealer
Dierden William, carman & farmer
Frost Samuel R. carpenter
Graves Thomas, draper
Gunn John Westacott, frmr. Manor fm
Hazel Robert, Blue Anchor P.H.; beanfeasts & tea parties catered for
Hudson John, Ingress Tavern P.H
Kent William, shopkeeper
Ladd Frank, baker
Martin Richard, beer retailer
Martin Wm. Edwd. baker & corn dlr
Matthews William, fried fish dealer
Moss Frederick, butcher
Norris George William, shopkeeper
Nugent Frances (Miss), girls' day school, Knockhall grove
Poole Henry, carpenter
Ramsay Frederick William, builder & undertaker, Ivy cottage
Ramsay John G. bldr. & contractr
Reid Alexander M.B., C.M. surgeon & certifying factory surgeon
Ridgewell Charles Thos. beer retailer
Ridgewell John, beer retlr. Milton st
Rixson Henry Joseph, confectioner
Saward John, shopkeeper
Sharpe James, beer retailer
Souten Joseph Stephen, shopkeeper, Knockhall
Souten Walter John, greengrocer & dairyman
Stevens Joseph, grocer
Wellard Walter, butcher
White John Bazley & Bros. Limited, portland & keen's cement & whiting manufacturers & brick makers; & at Stone, Rochester & Gillingham; chief offices, 2 Lime St.sq.Ludn EC
White Edward, sen. farmer
White Edward, jun. fruit grower
White John, dairyman
Wright William, boot maker

Page of Swanscombe from the 1899 Kellys Directory

Galley Hill & High Street

Postcard Photograph of Galley Hill 1905

This is a great view of Galley Hill and the High Street taken by Len Todd
from the chimney stack of the old white works in 1961

Gee's Tobacconists, High Street. This view is on the west side of the High Street near the George & Dragon. Most of the buildings dated from the 1850-1880 period, when the previously largely empty road grew rapidly with the cement workers' influx. Gee's shop was in operation from about 1912 to the 1950s, later selling sweets as well as tobacco. Hot cordials were provided at the shop for tram drivers in winter. These were prepared in the private apartment on the range with a black kettle. Sweets displayed in the window were in dishes with little paper doyleys. The Gee family themselves only allowed their children to eat boiled sweets, which were considered safe from diseases such as diphtheria.. (From Christoph Bull "Swanscombe in old picture postcards" 2005)

Same view, as above taken from London Road in 1910, notice Gee's Tobacconists from above is not yet in operation. To the left is All Saints and to the right out of shot is the George & Dragon.

Photograph of Galley Hill looking towards the George and Dragon

The only change here is the Victorian Houses which were demolished in 1977

And replaced by the Galley Hill Industrial Estate

High Street, Swanscombe circa 1935. A view looking north. In the background can be seen the ubiquitous cement factory chimney belching out the bane of the housewife - cement dust settled on washing as well as roofs and gardens. Swanscombe was still very self-contained despite bus and rail connections to elsewhere. The Kent Messenger shop shown (the proprietor was L G. Peacock) was were used by the few people who commuted to London - most locals worked in or around Swanscombe in the 1930s. Further down on the right was Albert Banks' Cycle Shop, which sold motorcycles and wirelesses (radios). It was a shop for recharging accumulators (heavy batteries used for powering electrical equipment) and car batteries could also be topped up from here. Behind All Saint's Church was its parish room, a wooden hut used by various clubs including one of the 'Slate Clubs', which meant weekly subscriptions of a few pennies, to build a fund for medical insurance in the days prior to the National Health Service. *(*From Christoph Bull "Swanscombe in old picture postcards" 2005)

Same view today 2011

Two more views of Galley Hill in 1930 and 2011

Co-Operative Society Shops, High Street. This view was taken around 1914 - the parade was opened in 1913. The 'CO-OP' symbolized the working class ideals of self help and it also shows that Swanscombe felt greater affinity with Gravesend and Northfleet rather than Dartford - if for no other reason than the trams ran direct to Gravesend. The Gravesend Co-Operative Society began its Swanscombe branch in about 1889 - it was in operation by 1891 – William John Francis then being the manager when it was situated in Broomfield Road. This building dominated (and still does) the upper part of the High Street in Galley Hill and contained (in 1937) a grocers, drapers and outfitters and a butcher in addition to halls above used numerous community groups and for wedding receptions. Everybody had a shop number during the war and you paid by dividend our family number was 9447. This building replaced two thatched cottages, which had burned down earlier. The Cooperative movement in Gravesend ceased in the 1980s, since when this building has been used by different shops. . *(*From Christoph Bull "Swanscombe in old picture postcards" 2005)

The old COOP building now used as charity shops 2011

Galley Hill Postcard 1910

Views of High Street - Galley Hill 2011

Picture Postcard High Street – Galley Hill c1930

Galley Hill/High Street Then & Now

The Parade of shops seen here was built in 1961 but before that were a row of 2up and 2down houses a shop which was a dry cleaners then a shop on the corner after a little driveway, which was run by Arthur Mercer. Then there was Ramsdales Dairy (see below) then a row of houses, on the end was Charlie Loveridge's Fish and Chip Shop. At the back of the shops Mr & Mrs Fuller kept pigs which in the summer gave a foul smell many people complained about the stink. Their son Robin Loveridge was a scout leader. Also at the back called the Grove where the Council office's and sports ground is today were two chalk pits which ran from the back of the dry cleaners, they were connected by a long tin bridge. Children would often play in the pits and get quite dirty when you found the safest way down into them that is. After the war the pits were filled in from the soil from Northfleet on a large conveyor belt this went on for quite some time. There after the ground was leveled built on.

Site of the old grove chalk pits now the council office and sports ground 2011

Old Post Office   Barbers and Bike Shop   to find out

After the Fish and Chip shop are a long row of 2up and 2down houses which are still there, was a alley way which at the back used to be Mr Morecroft ran a printers works, was the superintendent at the Wesleyan Methodist Chapel in Chruch Road, next to this was the site of the old post office, when the post office moved over the road it became a sweetshop then florist. Next door was a barber shop one upstairs and one down, upstairs was Mr Charlie Hudson and down was run by Mr Bill Parks. Next was Mr Hodges bike shop and accumulators recharger. Then the Wheatsheaf, the landlord was Les Dear who during the was a rear gunner in Lancaster Bomber who didn't say much about the war but always said he never hit a bloody thing. The next shop on this side of the road was the Cooperative.

Over the road.

Methodist Chuch

On a summers day on the 31st August 1887, at a meeting in Broomfield Road, six men sat down and had a meeting that a trust should be formed to build a Methodist Chapel, not exceeding a cost of £500.00. The Chapel was known as the primitive Methodist and the smaller Wesleyan Methodists also were in Church Road. The joining of the two chapels took place in 1937. The original persons involved in this were, Messrs Higgins, Edwins, Weirn, Grout. Bailey, Bare, Biggs, and more but these names are written in the minutes for the period around 1900.

CHANGES: Methodist Minister Rosemary Davies
ND/4237/28AC

Corner of Stanhope Road and High Street

Sallys Hairdressers
Kemps Provisions Shop

Second Hand Cloths Shop
Stokes Fish & Chip Shop
Sweetshop and Greencrocers

Galliards Buthers Shop
Wilkins Shoe Shop

Starting at Corner of Stanhope Road were Kemps Corners which contained Sallys Hairdressers, Kemps Groceries and Provisions, then Macdonalds Drapes. Coming round into High Street were Greengrocers next was a Sweetshop, then Frank Stokes Fish & Chip Shop, then next was the second hand cloths shop, next is Mr Wilkins shoe shop, Mr Galliards Butcher Shops which before that was Bonds Butcher shop.

Bond's Butcher Shop

Bond's Butcher Shop, High Street. A typical feature of any town or village was the butcher's shop. In the days before refrigeration the meat was displayed in the open air and if unsold during the day it would be often sold off very cheap or given away very late at night. Poorer families would wait until such times in order to obtain occasional meat in their diet. Like most shops, Bonds would slaughter their own stock with the resultant screams and rivers of blood in a densely populated area. A strange homemade flywheel sausage machine existed at the rear of the shop operated by both petrol and gas in the mid-1920s. Bonds operated from the premises at 62 High Street from about 1892 until 1918, then at 108 High Street until about 1921. Bonds also had another butcher's shop in Milton Road. . *(From Christoph Bull "Swanscombe in old picture postcards" 2005)*

Post Office

Whites Ironmonger
Mr Stan Crouch Sweetshop
Pearce Brothers Merchants

Mrs Fields café

The Post Office which was built in 1958 used to be the Old Forge which later catered for cars then in 1980 the front of the shop was used as a dry cleaners called Swanscombe Dry. Next in the row were Pearce Brothers corn and seed merchants next was Mr Stan Crouches sweetshop then Mrs Fields café which she ran for many years with the help of Mrs Harper.

The Forge, High Street. The garage of its time, the forge not only shoed horses but made and repaired almost any metalwork object. The forge shown here was a product of the industrial rather than the agricultural period, as its position in the High Street would have been an empty country lane until the 1850s. The forge was operated by Messrs. Bundy and Williams at the turn of the twentieth century and consisted of a yard, a building directly on the High Street and the smithy itself behind at the rear of the site. The forge had adapted to the end of the horse age by becoming the 'Old Forge Garages' where it repaired cars by the late 1930s. In 1938 the site was worked by Messrs. F. Axford and J.D. Love, who operated the garage, while Pearce Brothers, who were corn and seed merchants, also occupied the area. During the 1960s the whole site was redeveloped as an ugly new post office which itself became Swanscombe Dry Cleaners during the mid-1980s. . (From Christoph Bull "Swanscombe in old picture postcards" 2005)

Sorting Office 2011

Swanscombe Dry 1991

Addisons Tailors and Shoes Sid Colemans Barber Shop Coop and the Post Office 2005
Ostels Chemist Shop
Bampton & Simmonds Tool Shop

Harry's Fishmongers & Fish & Chips Shop Bookmakers Lowens Butcher Shop

Continuing up the High Street, the Tattooist was Addinsons Tailors and shoes they also sold Haberdashery next was Sid Colemans Barber shop, which later became the post office before it became part of the coop. Next was Mrs Ostel Chemists in the window she displayed all sorts of jars and bottles with stickers on them telling you what was in them, in the centre there were two large bowls one was green and one was red. Then there was a tool shop come ironmongers called Bampton & Simmonds. Then there was the very popular Harry's Fish and Chip shop, in this shop on one side he sold fish and chips on the other he sold wet fish and seafood. On the corners was the local betting office. On the other corners was Mr Lowens Butcher shop, he was also the scout master for the 1st Galley Hill 18th Gravesend Troop. Mr Theobold ran the 1st Swanscombe Troop

After the Butchers on the corner a little further on was the coop over the road as seen above were a Newsagents and a sweet shop run by Mr Brewer and a bit further down was Albert Banks Cycle Shop. There was one last shop in the High Street before you got to Gees Tobacconist was yet another Sweet Shop. Why Swanscombe had so many confectionary shops one can only guess.

High Street, Galley Hill, circa 1938. View looking North. The Galley Hill name still continued, even though this had long been considered Swanscombe High Street. The area was bristling with businesses in shops, which were often converted terraced houses. The pole on the right marks the barbershop of Frederick Homewood at this time. By looking at a local street directory in the late 1930s this one road had the following businesses: a tobacconist, confectioner, baker, co-operative society, two pubs, a general store, cycles, hairdressers, post office, printer, fishmonger and fish and chips, greengrocer, clothier, butcher, boot maker, corn and seed merchant, garage, laundry, hardware, chemist, optician, photographer and draper; several of these businesses had two different shops in the High Street alone. . *(From Christoph Bull "Swanscombe in old picture postcards" 2005)*

High Street 1950

'The Square', Swanscombe. Everyone who knows Swanscombe is aware that there has never been an area known as 'The Square'. The view is the junction of Stanhope Road into the High Street around 1935. The bus service had replaced the trams in 1929 and, unlike the trams, the buses had flexible routes down into Swanscombe itself instead of by passing the town along London Road which was the case with the trams. The Slabs or 'Squint Eye Row' cottages can be seen on the right of the picture, but it is Ramsdales Dairy, which dominated the view at this time. The dairy was formerly 'The Prince of Wales' public house, which ceased business around 1914 becoming one of the three dairies in Swanscombe, which survived into the late 1930s. The whole parade of shops including Ramsdale's Dairy and the neighbouring cottages in Milton Road (to the left) were demolished in 1961 and replaced by a red brick row of shops. This later development was designed to improve Swanscombe's shopping and made a major visual impact in an area of Victorian development. . *(From Christoph Bull "Swanscombe in old picture postcards" 2005)*

The new Parade of shops which replaced the old buildings. These were built in 1961

Same view as above taken 2011

Stanhope Road

Stanhope Road, Swanscombe circa 1930. The junction of Stanhope Road and the High Street as it was around 1930. It was then known as 'Kemp's Corner' as Kemp's grocery shop was directly on the junction. Macdonald's draper's shop then joined the buildings around into Stanhope Road itself. The houses on the left were known locally as "the Slabs' and also as 'Squint Eye Row' on account of the front parlours being different shapes in each house as to fit on the building plots as the road bent around the corner. As this area was often considered the centre of Swanscombe, the lamp-post in the picture was used to greet the New Year at midnight on 31 December, by people singing and socializing. . (From Christoph Bull "Swanscombe in old picture postcards" 2005)

Stanhope Road taken 2011

BelleVue House, Stanhope Road circa 1910. This house is unlike the workers cottages, which were rapidly covering Swanscombe from the 1840s onwards. Belle Vue was situated with views over the Ebbsfleet Valley towards Northfleet prior to the excavation of the land and before industrialization had covered the area. The sales particulars of a very similar building on Galley Hill show us that there was a handsome entrance hall with kitchens, wine cellar and coal cellar in the basement. The ground floor having two parlours with a water closet and a handsome staircase to the next floor with two good chambers: one front and one back complete with a neat dressing room with two roomy chambers on the top floor. A coach house with loft over came as part of the property as did gardens and the house was newly constructed in 1846. Swanscombe Urban District councilor Thomas Kemp lived here until the mid-1930s. During the Second World War the house was used as flats for bombed-out families and it has been a home for the elderly since the 1980s. During the interwar years tbe house next door was the home and practice of Dr. Michael Lynch, one of three general practitioners in Swanscombe at that time. . (From Christoph Bull "Swanscombe in old picture postcards" 2005)

Same view today 2011

Lodge Farm

Rixson's Farm Stanhope Road. This farmhouse was known as 'Lodge Farm' during the twentieth century and as 'Swanscombe Lodge' in the nineteenth century. The house contained much flint in addition to brickwork and probably dated from the eighteenth century before being altered in Victorian times. The farm occupied much of the land between Stanhope Road and the border with Northfleet, and was in the ownership of Mr. S.C. Umbreville of Ingress Abbey during the 1870s. William Rixson later occupied the farm, before he gave up the site in 1944. Lodge Farm had acres of orchards in the nineteenth century but its fields were steadily taken over as allotments so that Swanscombe locals could access extra food for themselves and by 1938 the rest of the farmland had been destroyed by chalk quarrying. The house was still able to sell some produce but soon became dilapidated. The farm was eventually demolished in 1984. . *(From Christoph Bull "Swanscombe in old picture postcards" 2005)*

Stanhope Road view taken 2011, showing Southfleet Road and Swan Valley School.

Church Road

Church Road, Swanscombe circa 1905. Church Road follows the line of an old footpath, which ran parallel to Stanhope Road linking the Galley Hill area with Swanscombe Village itself. Most of Church Road ran through fields and past hedgerows until the 1880s - only a few cottages and a small brewery and beer house, which was the original Morning Star public house, existed here before. This view shows Church Road before it was fully developed with housing - note the gas lamp-post and cottages on the left with no front gardens. Further up on the left, and the houses on the right, do have small gardens and these features give an indication of the respective rents and therefore the social mix of the tenants. The gap on the left is Harmer Road with its school opened in 1893, closed in 1967 and then used as a youth club before demolition in November 1998. Many of the gaps seen on the right side were filled with housing in the 1920s and 1930s. . (From Christoph Bull "Swanscombe in old picture postcards" 2005)

Church Road taken in 2011 few more cars in this photograph

Church Road, Swanscombe circa 1935. Church Road has been so called since the 1890s. Previously it had several names - originally known as Bird's Row and in the 1881 census it was called Barnfield Road, not becoming Church Road until after the Methodist chapel was built in 1888. In 1890 sale particulars list properties in Birds Row including a baker's shop (with parlour, kitchen scullery, four bedrooms and bakehouse with 10 bushel oven and storage over the top), and Ivy Cottage complete with coach house and stable, The road developed in a piece meal fashion. An example was in 1911 when local builder F.W Ramsay built two terraced houses for William Jenns at a cast of £349 4/-, these were numbers 8 and 10 Church Road, while seven cottages built between 105 and 117 Church Road were constructed in the 1920s by Sargeants - a Northfleet builder. Even this view displays various styles and ages of housing showing the hap hazard way it was developed. . (From Christoph Bull "Swanscombe in old picture postcards" 2005)

Same view as above taken in 2011

Church Road Shops

Walter Ames' shops, Church Road circa 1920. Walter Ames was a leading light in Swanscombe's civic as well as its economic affairs. By 1907 Ames had already established a considerable business empire, and by 1937 it covered the premises 88-98 Church Road. Ames was a boot and shoe dealer, clothier, draper, general warehouse, grocer and he ran Church Road post office. In his early years he is also listed as a baker. In 1894, when Swanscombe Parish Council was established, Walter Ames became its first chairman, an honour repeated in 1926 when he was the first chairman of the new Swanscombe Urban District Council. Ames was described as short with a well-groomed beard. He was well liked, very well known and seen as a man of action. Ames died in 1934 and was described as the 'Father of Swanscombe Council'.. (From Christoph Bull "Swanscombe in old picture postcards" 2005)

Walter Ames shop is now a private residents 2 views of Akers Chemist 2011 and 1991 and the end shop W Ames c 1930's

Church Road had a large number of business at one time these included 2 Garages 2 Churches 1 Pub, Starting from Swanscombe Street end shops which were here in 1940's were. Sid Hudson Barber Shop, Mrs Nelly Cramp Sweet Shop and Tobacconist, Mrs & Mrs Cooper ran the Morning Star when rebuilt. The Scouts Hall was a Wesleyan Methodist Chapel, an oblong building with a door on the side, which had a stage inside. Over the road was Church Road Service Garage, next to the church was another car repairs shop, opposite this was a coal yard which later became a fruit sellers which delivered. On the corner of Ames Road was Mr Pallants Greengrocers, then Walter Ames and Akers as above, opposite was S Allen Bakers 91 Church Road, then Thomas Flints Greengrocers 27 Church Road, next was Mrs Mays newsagents and sweetshop 29 Church Road, next Thomas Humphries boot and shoe repairs 39 Church Road, then the Fire Station/Library and the Methodist Church.

Swanscombe Street

Swanscombe Street looking East circa 1908. On the right side is the fence of Manor Farm, which stood next to St. Peter and St. Paul's Church (see Manor Farm). The farm had been owned by the cement industry since 1872 and was rented by a succession of farmers including John Westacott Gunn who ran it from about 1898 with the Gunn Family in occupation throughout the period prior to 1939. On the left is Eglington Road with a gas lamp-post supplied by the Northfleet and Greenhithe Gas Company. The row of Victorian terraced houses sweeps down to the Blue Anchor public house and its adjacent eighteenth century cottages. Beyond the Blue Anchor is what appears to have once served as the inn's stabling facilities before the early nineteenth century houses known as Rosina Terrace begin. Tasteless redevelopment since the 1960s has destroyed this scene apart from the now much altered Victorian cottages on the left. . (From Christoph Bull "Swanscombe in old picture postcards" 2005)

View of Swanscombe Street taken in 2011 notice the Blue Anchor public house has been rebuilt and moved back, and the Manor House and then Council offices have also gone now a playing field.

Swanscombe Street looking west circa 1905. The view is looking from the junction of Stanhope/Southfleet roads along Swanscombe Street. Like many streets, this has had several names. In 1881 it was Church Road, which is logical as the parish church is further along, but by 1909 it was 'High Street' and became Swanscombe Street shortly afterwards. . *(*From Christoph Bull "Swanscombe in old picture postcards" 2005)

Swanscombe Street view taken 2011

Blue Anchor Public House, Swanscombe Street, c1905. Swanscombe has had at least 25 pubs that are recorded - that excludes Greenhithe. Most public houses were 'beer houses' offering a basic service with no spirits allowed for sale. The Blue Anchor and the George & Dragon were the two premier establishments with full licenses and able to offer stabling for horses and rooms for guests. The name Blue Anchor is supposed to come from an ancient legend whereby a chain appeared from the sky one Sunday morning with an anchor at the end, which had lodged itself behind a gravestone in the churchyard. A man in sailor's costume descended the chain and in attempting to free the anchor drowned - even though he was on dry land. The chain was cut leaving him in Swanscombe. A local version of this story was that he was abandoned by the unseen vessel in the clouds, but survived to be the first landlord of the Blue Anchor. The anchor was seized by the locals, melted down and made into the hinges on the north door of St. Peter and St. Paul's church. This wonderful building, with astonishing lack of taste, was demolished and replaced with a new pub on the same site (but set further back from the road) in March 1965.
. *(From Christoph Bull "Swanscombe in old picture postcards" 2005)*

Blue Anchor Public House 1950 and 2011

Blue Anchor public house, Swanscombe Street. This photograph was taken at a time of transition - Style & Winch were taken over by Courage Brewery in 1958 and both companies are still displayed. The pub was built circa 1735 in what was the original village of Swanscombe, long before the days of Galley Hill's growth in the Victorian era. Like all pubs, the Blue Anchor hosted many local organisations such as the Royal Ancient Order of Buffalos, which is a friendly society for working class people to pay small amounts of money weekly and to use in case of illness or other crises. Swanscombe United Football Club also used the premises for their headquarters. The Hazel Family were landlords from the 1890s until the early 1980s. This view shows a small entrance on the right, which led into a yard and then onto a huge 158-foot-long garden with three outside toilets. A stable was situated to the right of the above entrance just out of the photograph) and a skittle alley was also part of the back building complex.
(From Christoph Bull "Swanscombe in old picture postcards" 2005)

Bottom of Swanscombe Street c1930 and 2011 below

Swanscombe Street was one of the main streets in the village as it was once known, this was the old High Street until Galley Hill became the centre of Swanscombe

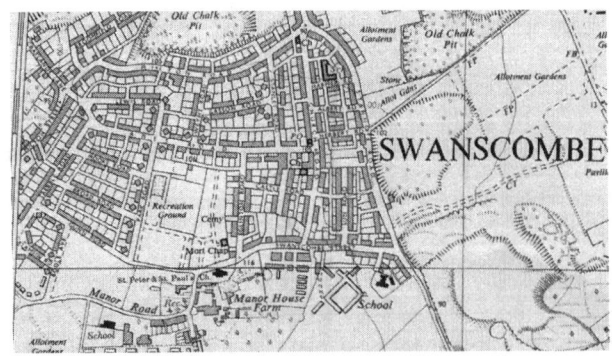

Southfleet Road

Southfleet Road c1930

Southfleet Raad, Swanscombe circa 1930. The view shows the twelve properties built after the sale of the land along the western edge of Southfleet Road in 1891. Originally a row of some 32 houses and shops was to occupy a great length of the road but most were never constructed. The Swan Valley School grounds occupy the site of the un-built houses but this small row had one shop in it: WJ. Pring, which was a general shop also selling sweets. The locals of the 1930s would wander down Southfleet Road to look at the newly -constructed 3-lane A2 and see the traffic on a Sunday night. Mr. Pring's shop was one of the few businesses open on a Sunday night to supply the needs of local traffic spotting: a custom that has long since lost its appeal in this age of almost universal car ownership. *(From Christoph Bull "Swanscombe in old picture postcards" 2005)*

Southfleet Road 2011

Moores Brothers
By Swanscombe Women Volume 2

Moore Brothers Mineral Water Factory in Broomfield Road

MOORES' MINERAL WATERS
Famous since 1879
Moore Bros, (Swanscombe) Ltd,   Swanscombe

1931 Advert

Moores Mineral Waters was formed in 1879, but was started in 1870 by, Mr John Baker, he sold home made ginger beer in stone bottles, which he would sell from wooden cart pulled by a donkey. His brother Mr Joseph Baker was also involved in the business as a partner. They built a small factory in what was Goreham Villa, which was opposite Galley Hill School. In 1879 Mr James Moore the grandfather of Mr Edward Moore (former councilor) offered to by the his part of the business from Joseph Baker, which he accepted. When James Moore passed away his widow Emily Moore purchased John Baker's remaining part, thus becoming sole proprietor. A horse and van were used to distribute the bottles to its customers, upon her two elder sons entered into running the business.

A large factory was acquired in Broomfield Road when the business began to grow and became successful, another building was built in Milton Road, near what is now Kingsdale Court ,which at the time was mainly arable farm land and orchards. The two elder sons then set up factories in Bromley and Weymouth, which increased the company's profile even more. The factory was extended firstly in 1912 then again in 1918, after war the factory was added to thereafter. The late Mr George Moore was killed in the first daylight raid over North Kent in August 1940 at Northfleet and his nephew, Edward Moore, took over. During the war, it became a hub producing unit for soft drinks, covering a wide area in Kent and the South East of London. The business was under control of the Ministry of Food and it was not until 1946 that the business could carry on where it left of and once again became a top brand. Moore's had around ten employees they wore clogs and very heavy rubber aprons, over which they had thick sacking to keep them dry, while they cleaned the bottles for reuse.

Moore Brothers created the Brand "AMBA" which sold names such as Kitty Cola, Keg Shandy, Wonder Orange. However by the late 1960's competition from UK and USA began to take its toll on the company so after 93 years of trading Moore Brothers ceased trading in 1973.

Milton Road & Milton Street Junction

March Past of the Brotherhood Brass Band c1936

Brotherhood Band Milton Road, Swanscombe, c1936. Part of the Gravesend and North Kent Hospital Carnival- a fund raising annual event which snaked its route via Swanscombe and Greenhithe on to Northfleet and Gravesend. The shop in the picture is that of F.V Jones, a general shop selling groceries and greengroceries as well. One of Swanscombe's three police constables (P.C William Sage) lived in the fifth house after the shop. At the very end of the terrace was a single story building, which had been a private school known as the 'Kirteen' Private School, which was in operation by 1887 but had closed by 1906. The band was one of many in Swanscombe - this one from one of the many chapels in the town.
(From Christoph Bull "Swanscombe in old picture postcards" 2005)

Milton Road 2011

Milton Street taken in c1914

Milton Street, Swanscombe circa 1914. A view looking south-west. On the right stand the Victorian houses known as 'Pustwell Villas' (dated 1898) with Victorian terraced houses on both sides of the road dating from the 1890s and early 1900s. The houses on the right were all destroyed on 27th February 1945 (V2 rocket), killing eight people and injuring 48 - only one house survived. The street is still mud but gas lamp-posts show the increasing urbanisation of the area. The white house in the centre of this picture is the Swanscombe Consolidated Almshouse Charity which has its origins in numerous sixteenth- to nineteenth-century parish bequests for the poor which were amalgamated to create this dwelling for four poor people. The house was opened in 1911 and was subsequently refurbished in 1980. The final house is a thatched Kentish weatherboard house of the late seventeenth or eighteenth century and consists of two dwellings. Buildings such as these were very common in most local villages but they were seen as 'slums' and lacking in modern amenities - especially after the 1920s, when they were mercilessly demolished by local authorities. The last of these types of cottages in Swanscombe were demolished in November 1971. . *(From Christoph Bull "Swanscombe in old picture postcards" 2005)*

View of Milton Street 2011

Thatch Cottage, Milton Street. A closer look at the two Kentish weatherboard cottages, seen in the previous picture. In the background can be seen Milton Street snaking its way towards Manor Road and Alkerden Lane. The Woodman public house can just be seen behind, which closed 1913-1914. As mentioned the last of these types of cottages survived until 1971 when, with the usual complete absence of imagination by the planners, they were demolished. The open country seen in the background of this picture is now covered with housing such as Alamein Road, built in the later 1940s, and Child's Crescent, Wallace Gardens and Wright Close, built in the 1950s. Behind the cottages are apple orchards with a notice warning against trespassing as' gintraps' await thieves . *(*From Christoph Bull "Swanscombe in old picture postcards" 2005)

Milton Street taken in c1930

Milton Road crossroads taken in c1950, the bus in the picture is most likely the 488, which route went via Church Road and the 487, which went via Milton Road both buses went into Gravesend.

Milton Road and Milton Street, was a very busy place in the 1930/40/50's with a wide variety of shops the locals would use. Milton Road started at the Parade in the High Street and finished at the roundabout. On the way were Moores Brothers Mineral Drinks Company which is now town houses, after this was Long Hut which had the air-raid siren on top, and children would watch a picture show inside. Then there was Mrs Jones Sweet Shop, which is now Monarchs Garage. Then Mr Todds scrap yard, in Broomfield Road was a off license which was run by the Uings Brothers called "The Fort" on the other side of the road were, Sid Colemans Barbers then, Mrs Kingsbury grocer shop. On the corner was Stan Akers other Chemist and a Provisions Store. Over the road were Thompson's Butchers, a newsagents run by Jack Wayne former policeman.

Milton Road, Swanscornbe, circa 1920. The lamp-post supplied by Northfleet & Greenhithe Gas Works is strategically placed at the junction of the High Street, Church Road and Milton Road. Discussions were held in 1854 for the provision of streetlights in Swanscombe and they were in operation by the late nineteenth century. The row of cottages on the right was demolished in about 1961 to make way for the rash of 1960s shops. Further along on the right are the two shops of Mr. Mercer (owner of the cinema and local councillor) and Harry Town (fruiter and dairy) - the latter had an early public telephone. On the left is the corner of the Primitive Methodist Church with a dozen cottages beyond which were open fields looking across towards Milton Street. The open ground was developed by Swanscombe Urban District Council in its campaign to improve housing within the town and the roads of Ames, Gasson, Stanley and Sweyne all now cover this area. Ames, Gasson and Stanley are all named after Swanscombe councillors and the roads were in existence by 1929. . (From Christoph Bull "Swanscombe in old picture postcards" 2005)

Fire Brigade in carnival, Milton Road, Swanscombe circa 1929. The photograph was taken at almost the same point as the previous two photographs and is part of the Gravesend and North Kent Hospital Carnival- a time of great community involvement in raising money essential for the hospital's maintenance. Swanscombe sent its patients to the hospital at Gravesend, rather than Dartford. The first fire engine was the horse-drawn manual pump purchased around 1903. Behind it appears to be the Garfield converted vehicle used by the fire brigade in the 1920s until replaced in 1930.The horse-drawn engine was only used on occasions such as this and its replacement was a Fiat vehicle, which appears to have retained the hand pump equipment from the horse-drawn engine. The flat was sold to Hoo St.Werburgh Parish Council as their fire engine in 1930 for £10. . (From Christoph Bull "Swanscombe in old picture postcards" 2005)

Craylands Lane

Craylands Lane, Swanscombe circa 1902. A view looking north from the junction with Milton Street. The pub on the right side (at end of row of cottages) was the Rising Sun - the only survivor of three public houses along this road. On the left is a Victorian detached house, which stood on the site of a farm yard, which had barns and a hop kiln in the 1860s. During the 1930s it was used by Stone Court Ballast Company, but it is now demolished. The barn further along is the last survival of the farmyard of Crown Farm and behind the barn was one of the many allotments in Swanscombe. The present-day Swanscombe Centre (which did include the Swanscombe & GreenhitheTown Council offices) was opened in 1989 on a site to the left of the cart shown in the picture. . *(From Christoph Bull "Swanscombe in old picture postcards" 2005)*

Craylands Lane 2011

CalvaryTerrace, Craylands Lane, Swanscombe circa 1905. Craylands Lane is an ancient road linking the hamlet of Milton Street with the main Gravesend to Dartford road (A226) at Swanscombe Cross, directly opposite to the main entrance to the Cement Works. This area was developed by the needs of the cement workers and the houses dated from the 1850s and 1860s. It was developed into a little community with 3 public houses two are shown here. On the extreme left is the Coopers Arms (known locally as the 'Bottom House'). The large building on the right of the picture (next to the alleyway) was the North Kent (known as the 'Middle House') and beyond that, towards Milton Street, was the Rising Sun (the 'Top House') - outside of this view. All 3 pubs were in operation until after the Second World War - only the Rising Sun remains. The alleyway. seen next to the North Kent led to Craylands Square, another Victorian creation consisting of some 15 or so small cottages and houses. This whole area was redeveloped in the very early 1970s and replaced by housing of that period. . (From Christoph Bull "Swanscombe in old picture postcards" 2005)

plied by the Metropolitan Water Board. The ecclesiastical parishes of All Saints, Swanscombe, and of St. Mary the Virgin, Greenhithe, are included in the urban district; particulars will be found under the separate headings of GALLEY HILL and GREENHITHE respectively. The church of SS. Peter and Paul is a building chiefly in the Early English style, with a tower and steeple, but there are parts showing Saxon and Norman work, notably a double splayed Saxon window; on August 13, 1902, the church was struck by lightning and much damage was done by fire; most of the woodwork was renewed including the shingled broach spire: there are monuments to the Weldons, including those of Anthony Weldon, Eleanor, his wife, and on the south side a monument of alabaster with recumbent effigies of their son, Sir Ralph Weldon kt. ob. 1609, a knight in armour and his lady, both resting their heads on pillows: the nave and aisles were restored by Sir James Erasmus Wilson LL.D., F.R.S. who formerly lived here, died in 1884, and was buried in the church; a stained window commemorates the restoration, and there are four others, including one erected to the memory of the men of this parish who fell in the Great War, 1914-18; their names are inscribed on an oak mural tablet. The register dates from the year 1559. The living is a rectory, net yearly value £692, with 3 acres of glebe and residence, in the gift of Sidney Sussex College, Cambridge, and held since 1917 by the Rev. Edward Francis Campbell Ward M.A. of that college, hon. canon of Rochester. There is a Methodist chapel, a Congregational chapel at INGRESS VALE, built in 1860, with 300 sittings, and a Baptist meeting room at Milton street. A burial ground was formed in 1885 at a cost of £493, and has since been thrice extended; it has a mortuary and chapel, and is under the control of the Council. A fire station was erected in 1908 and extended in 1920, and is also under the control of the Council. Beare's Almshouses, founded in 1587 by John Beare, of Greenhithe, for six old persons (female), are situated at Greenhithe; the inmates are supported chiefly from a charity left in 1721 by Lady Judith Swan, and endowed with half an acre of land, which is let on building and other leases. The income is about £137 a year; each inmate over 70 years of age receives 3s. 4d. per week, and those under 70, 5s. 6d. per week. A new almshouse was erected in 1911, containing eight rooms, for four aged couples, each of whom receives 1s. a week. Swanscombe Wood is well known; and there is a cavern called "Clabbernappers Hole."

The extensive cement works of the Associated Portland Cement Manufacturers Ltd. are at Swanscombe Cross, and there are paper mills at Greenhithe. The Ebbsfleet stream was formerly navigable. Swanscombe manor house, an ancient building, and the seat of the Weldon family, is now occupied as a farm house. The Associated Portland Cement Manufacturers Ltd. and the trustees of the late Thomas Colyer esq. are the principal landowners. The soil is gravel and chalk; subsoil, chalk. The area is 2,142 acres of land and inland water; the population in 1931 was 8,543. The population of the wards in 1931 was:—Galley Hill, 2,221; Greenhithe, 2,547; Swanscombe, 3,775. The population of the ecclesiastical parish of SS. Peter and Paul in 1931 was 4,129.

GALLEY HILL and GREENHITHE will be found under separate headings.

KNOCKHALL, half a mile west; Western Cross, three-quarters of a mile south-west; Milton Street, a quarter of a mile north-west; and Alkerden, half a mile south-west, are hamlets.

URBAN DISTRICT COUNCIL.

Offices, Manorway house, London road.
Council meets third tuesday at 7.30 p.m.

Members.
Chairman, P. Fletcher.
Vice-Chairman, T. Bodle.

A. S. Allen
R. Barlass
M. J. Cox
W. J. Everard
S. J. Fright
John E. Gunn J.P
E. Hills
J. E. Hollis

W. A. Knight
A. W. Lane
George Moore
Rev. S. Morgan C.C
G. H. Sparkes
A. J. Talbot
W. J. Webb
C. E. E. Wellman

Officials.
Clerk & Accountant, Harold Tuffee
Deputy Clerk, W. R. James
Collector & Rating Officer, F. G. Peters
Surveyor-Inspector, L. E. Croucher
Treasurers, Barclays Bank Ltd. (Northfleet branch)
Medical Officer, C. M. Ockwell M.D.Lond., F.R.C.S.Eng., L.R.C.P.Lond., D.P.H.Camb

Town, Sub-Post, M. O. & T. Office. Letters through Greenhithe

PRIVATE RESIDENTS.

(For T N's see general list of Private Residents at end of book.)
Blackman Mrs. 19 Knockhall grove
Fletcher P. 2 Milton road
Gunn John Edwin J.P. Manor house
Harley William, 15 Knockhall grove
Lane A. W., J.P. 16 Park road
Lynch Michael Francis B., M.B., B.S. Lond. Stanhope road
Ward Rev. Canon Edward Francis Campbell M.A. (rector), Rectory

COMMERCIAL.

Marked thus ° farm 150 acres or over.
Acker Stanley, chemist, 137a, Milton rd
Adams Bessie (Miss), ladies' hairdresser, Stanley rd
Allen Arth. S. baker, 91 Church road
Ames Wltr. grocer, & post office, Church rd. Gravesend 1662
Associated Portland Cement Manufacturers Ltd
Barker Wm. shopkpr. Eglington rd
Blue Anchor P.H. (Wm. Hazel)
Brice-Baker Herbt. dentist (attends mon. & fri.), 89 Church rd
Brind Chas. Rt. coal dlr. 148 Church rd. Gravesend 1630
Butler Nellie (Mrs.), shopkpr. Church rd
Cassingham Albt. local secretary for Tunbridge Wells Equitable Friendly Society, 106 Stanhope rd
Cemetery (W. E. Neale, supt)
Church Road Service Garage, Church rd
Churcher A. & Son, bakers, 18 Swanscombe st
Clout C. T. & A. shopkprs. 67 Knockhall rd
Crouch Roy & Ronald, boot reprs. Stanley rd
Farr Hy. E. shopkpr. 90 Stanhope rd
Filmer Saml. Chas. shopkpr. Milton rd
Fletcher Peter, dairyman, 2 Milton rd
Flint Thos. fruitr. 27 Church rd
Frost Albt. Edwd. undertaker, 64 Stanhope rd. T N Gravesend 701
°Gunn Jn. Edwin J.P. farmer, Manor farm. Gravesend 450
Hardy Fredk. Chas. G. grocer, 2 Stanhope rd
Harling Albt. Edwd. confctnr. Stanley rd
Harris Jn. Sydney, plasterer, 16 Stanhope rd
Humphrey Alfd. Thos. boot & shoe repr. 39 Church rd
Hutson Charles G. hair dresser, 54 Swanscombe street
Ingress Tavern (Arth. Ludlow), Knockhall rd. Greenhithe 78
°Kemsley J. Thos. farmer, Western Cross. Greenhithe 1
Kingsbury Wm. Jn. cooked meat dlr. 127 Milton rd
Leaman Lucy (Mrs.), shopkpr. 20 Sun rd
Lynch Michl. Fras. B., M.B., B.S. Lond. physcn. & surgn. (firm, Lynch & Morgan), Stanhope rd. Gravesend 434
Macdonald Malcolm Ronald, draper, 4 Stanhope road
May Alice M. (Mrs.), shopkpr. 29 Church rd
May Geo. & Son, butchers, Church rd
Moore Bros. mineral water manufacturers. T N Gravesend 444
Morning Star P.H. (Mrs. Eliz. Orum), Church rd
Openshaw Catherine (Miss), shopkpr. 128 Church rd
Pallant J. D. & Sons, fruitrs. 100 Church rd. Gravesend 953
Palmer Emma C. (Mrs.), secondhand furniture dlr. 58 Swanscombe st
Piper Lawrence, insur. agt. 147 Knockhall rd
Pring T. J. & Sons, greengrocers, 2 Swanscombe street
Pring Wltr. G. confctnr. 9 Southfleet rd
Ramsdale Wm. Rt. dairy, 2 Milton rd
Rixson Brenda (Mrs.), shopkpr. 112 Stanhope rd
Rixson Fredk. Ernest, haulage contrctr. 4a, Swanscombe st. Gravesend 1710
Shell-Mex & B.P. Ltd. corner of Craylands ln. & London rd. Gravesend 666
Snow Winifred (Mrs.), shopkpr. 22 Swanscombe st
Spooner Sidney, fruitr. 123 Milton rd
Sun P.H. (Hy. A. Tyler), Swanscombe st
Swanscombe Transport Co. Ltd. haulage contrctrs. High st. Gravesend 1496
Swanscombe Urban District Council Fire Brigade (Hy. Lines, capt.), Church rd
Taylor L. (Mrs.), fishmngr. Stanley rd
Thompson Jemima (Mrs.), butcher, Castle st. Gravesend 89x
Tickle Ralph, farmer, Stanhope road
Watson Chas. Fredk. shopkpr. 1 Eglinton rd

Cartoon Sketch of Swanscombe Traders and Shop Keepers 1939
By Mickey Durling

Swanscombe Galley Hill & High Street Shop Map 1930

	LONDON ROAD	
GEORGE AND DRAGON PUB	G	
GEES TOBACCONIST	A	ALL SAINTS CHURCH
GUNNERS BAKERS	L	
PRIVATE HOUSE	L	CHURCH HALL
PRIVATE HOUSE	E	
PRIVATE HOUSE	Y	
PRIVATE HOUSE		
ROGERS SWEETSHOP	H	
	I	
	L	RAILWAY PLATFORM AND PATH
RAILWAY LINE	L	RAILWAY LINE
	RAILWAY BRIDGE	RAILWAY PLATFORM AND PATH
PATH		RAILWAY STATION
		PRIVATE HOUSE
THE ALMA PUB	H	NEWSAGENT
	I	COOKSHOP AND GREENGROCERS
PRIVATE HOUSE	G	PRIVATE HOUSE
PRIVATE HOUSE	H	PRIVATE HOUSE
PRIVATE HOUSE		ARGENTINE BUTCHERS
PRIVATE HOUSE	S	STEVENS CYCLE SHOP AND COFFEE SHOP
COOP BUTCHERS	T	PRIVATE HOUSE
COOP SHOP	R	PRIVATE HOUSE
COOP GREENGROCERS	E	PRIVATE HOUSE
COOP DRAPER	E	PRIVATE HOUSE
PRIVATE HOUSE	T	
PRIVATE HOUSE		
PRIVATE HOUSE		FORDHAMS BUTCHERS
PRIVATE HOUSE		
THE GROVE ALLEYWAY		ALLEY
THE WHEATSHEAF PUB		CATTONS BAKERS
SQUANCE HARDWARE	H	LEE'S SHOE SHOP
HODGES CYCLE/TOY SHOP	I	CHURCH'S DRAPERS
PARKS BARBERS	G	PROVISIONS
SWEETSHOP AND SUB POST OFFICE	H	GOLDINGS BUTCHERS
MORECROFT PRINTERS		OSTLES CHEMIST
AVIS	S	HANDY JACKS HARDWARE
PRIVATE HOUSE	T	WHITE'S GREENGROCER
PRIVATE HOUSE	R	WILKINSONS SHOESHOP
PRIVATE HOUSE	E	COOKS CORN SHOP
PRIVATE HOUSE	E	THE FORGE
PRIVATE HOUSE	T	SKINNERS BUTCHERS
PRIVATE HOUSE		WARNERS SHOE SHOP
PRIVATE HOUSE		STOKES FISH SHOP
PRIVATE HOUSE		PRIVATE HOUSE
PRIVATE HOUSE		HOMEWOOD BARBER
EWELLES BUTCHERS		PRIVATE HOUSE
PRIVATE HOUSE		PRIVATE HOUSE
PRIVATE HOUSE		PRIVATE HOUSE
PRIVATE HOUSE		PRIVATE HOUSE
RAMSDALES DAIRY	LAMP STANDARD	GREEN'S COAL YARD
MILTON ROAD		STANHOPE ROAD
	CHURCH ROAD	KEMPS CORNER & McDONALDS DRAPERY

The Good Old Days
A Selection of Memoirs taken in 1972 by Sweyne School

By Mrs E Fenning (nee Lee)

Where to start, well I was born in Betsham on the 14th June 1888 I was fifth in line of a family of 9, 7 boys and 2 girls, a sister who died aged 8. I was the elder. The cottage where I was born still stands and I can remember going to Southfleet School with my brothers along wavey wall also called drunken mans alley, from Betsham. My parents were in the church choir in their youth, and my father was also a houseboy in the big house. When we left to go to Swanscombe we went to New Barn just at the bottom of Southfleet Road just past the where the A2 is now, we started school in the September and had to walk everyday there and back from New Barn to "Flint College" or Manor Road as it is called today. At New Barn we had to fetch water from the spring in the watercress fields near the Ebbsfleet River but we enjoyed it. The farmer at the time was Mr Ashby and my brother Elvey was their houseboy (servent). Our neighbours then were the Wakemens and Ravens. I remember this, as we had to share a "Privey" (outside toilet).

Then we moved again to Alkerden Farm, my father worked there for Mr J W Gunn for 25 years. My sister and baby brother died shortly after we moved there, it hit my mother hard but in those days it was quite common. Laura died of diptheria which was quite prevalent at the time. The one and only drain was found to be the cause. So the council at the time had it blocked up and thereafter everything has to be thrown over the wall into the yard where the cows, and horses, ducks, chickens, geese. We used to collect all the eggs and then we youngsters had to bring them up to Manor Farm, we would then be rewarded for our efforts with a penny. Opposite the house which had the yard was often flooded with water from "Newn Hill", which has since gone, at the back of the barn was a pond which during winter would freeze, then we would slide on it. The pond was really a duck pond!.

At the age of 13 I left school, having received a prize for buttonhole making and being in a concert, The award was to have a dress made my a proper dressmaker. It was marvelous, my mother was a very good needleworker and was done all by hand. But that pretty white dress was perfect to me as I had never had a dress made for me before.

The teachers at Manor Road at the time were Miss Cannon and Miss Carter, but the highlight came when we had a new Headmaster, Mr Peters, to us he was something quite out of the ordinary. As far as I can remember our only way of enjoyment was what we made ourselves, going on picnics to Springhead to see the monkeys and buy a large bunch of watercress for about 3d, walks to Greenhithe. I stayed home for a few years, to help my mother but in the end I got a job in Milton Road with a Doctor who was just starting, he was assistant to Dr Richmond of Greenhithe. They had two daughters and from 7am to 7pm, I was on call for 2s.6d. a week. I worked away with them but after 6 months I got home sick and came back to Swanscombe.

I looked around for another job and few months later I was working as a nursemaid for a Lady in the village with three children, I was being paid £12 per year, I was allowed to use the Lady's sewing machine and bicycle. One day a month, one evening a week and every other Sunday off, in by 9.30am only to find washing up to do. The along came world war 1, I had been then for 5 years and they left for Sidcup. By this time I was courting my husband to be, he worked for a high class grocers. He would leave every morning with his horse and van, how he loved his horses. Well war put that to a stop. We were married in April 1916 and by April 1917 we was in the Army training at Blackheath with the A.S.A. Our son was born in the October 1917 and his father stayed for a brief weekend, in April 1918 he was in France in the trenches and on 6th September 1918 he was killed. My five brothers all came home my sailor brother had been invalided home from Salonica he died in 1940 from his injuries.

So I had to start again, I had been drawing 12s.6d. per week pension, when my son was born it was increased to 17s.6d. I went back to work, my mother in law was good to me and my parents, but money was tight in those days. My son started school at Southfleet Road School but shortly afterwards my parents moved from Alkerden Farm to Milton Road and we found a haven at last. We lived there for 17 years. Than came the Second World War, my son was working in Wilmington Nursery. Then eventually he joined the army as a dispatch rider with the 8th Army.

I went full circle and ended up in a flat in Betsham.

By Mrs Grace Roots

I was born in the Grove, called half crown row as that was the price of the rent in 1885. I went to Galley Hill School. One morning a week we divided for scripture, Church lessons we taken by the vicar, and chapel was taken by the Ingress Vale minister. I remember while at school the River Thames flooded and the sea wall broke, a poor lad who was unlucky to be playing around the marshes at the time was drowned. The Thames flooded regular as this was before the modern sea wall was built in 1960's. During the depression money was hard to find, so it was decided to open a soup kitchen up at Church House, this went on for some years before things improved. The Church House became the 17th Club, which was opposite the George and Dragon, it was a similar building to Factory House in Northlfeet High Street but slightly smaller, outside were the toilets which are still there now, Inside on the first floor was a large dance area where we used to have dances and party's, the bar was at one end. Downstairs was turned into a Snooker club.

17th Club Badge   Swanscombe Bowling Club Badge   1937 Coronation Medal

Highlights was Sunday School treats when we marched behind bands for tea and games in the field, the band of hope and Sunday Schools were well attended. If you done well at school you sat for an exam at 11 years old, you then got a labour certificate and then left. I got my certififcate and then got a job at 6d a week delivering dinners to works. For that 6d would buy you, 1lbs sugar, quarter lb tea, half a pint of milk, or 2lbs

When old enough I went to work at the vicarage, I worked with a cook and housemaid, it was against the house rules to bring a boyfriend as this was not allowed, I had to warn and hide any young men in the cupboard if by any chance any of the family came home.

My mother took me to visit our old neighbour in the workhouse, she was dressed in a cotton frock, with a mop cap, sitting on a hard wooden chair, no comfort at all,

I married in 1909. Being a housewife was a full time job as with lamps and candles for lighting as we had no electricity then. Flues to clean, mop floors, coppers for washing cloths, no hot running water. And the men working nearly all day and night.

It was a time when everybody helped each other, if anyone fell on hard times a concert was given with local talent and the proceeds given to help out. Church and Chapel were well attended and social evenings arranged. Leisure time was spent walking and musical evenings in homes. Election time was always quite an event and everybody who was interested attended meetings.

After two wars the place has changed and grown so much. Looking back we were healthy happy, we walked every where, we didn't really need anything apart from everyday things. I seen the beginning of cars, planes, telephones, petty much everything that today people take for granted but to us it was a wonder and a spectacle.

It was a wonderful age to live through and some good and some bad, but Swanscombe when I was young was a little village surrounded with countryside on three sides and the river on the other side. Don't get me wrong it was hard, people died young and from lots of things you can cure today, but it was a simple time and I loved it.

Grace Roots (1972)

Swanscombe in the Past   By Mrs Stone

My earliest memory of Swanscombe, was when I was seven when I first walked to school by myself, The first memory is Harmer Road School. On the opposite side if the road were freshly ploughed fields and which were then planted, us kids would climb through the wire and run across the fields for a short cut home, otherwise we went round down the road past the Methodist Chapel and round the corner to Broomfield Road. The side of the road were starting to fill up with houses, and in 1908 they built the Fire Station as a one storey building and eventually Church Road emerged as it is today. And the land at the back remained as smaller fields with hedgerows boarding the lane, but as the years have passed this has all been built on with houses and is now known as Milton Street.

From Harmer Road School I then went to Manor Road School, so my journey took me past Woodman Road, now known as Milton Street, until I came to the footpaths know as the "Walks". These I walked along and came to the school by going through a short path out of the long one. Of course you could go straight on and you would reach the St Peter and St Paul Church and the old Farm oast buildings, with the rectory on one side of the cemetery on the other. Only the church and cemetery remain, new houses and a clinic have been built and lower down the new council offices.

We have a nice park, the top part takes the place of the "Daisy Field", where we used to go in and play, we would take our picnics and tea there. You had to down past the daisy field to get through the turnstiles to enter the football field. We also had sports meetings for several years and were a wonderful highlight in our little community. The first was held in 1909, as when I was 13 I ran in some races, and the excitement of the tug-of-war, my father was a local team trainer, and was very successful, winning the cup with the "Chalkies" (Swanscombe United) team.

They were happy times with no hint of the two wars that were to follow. But as the years passed all parts of our lovely little village altered or have been demolished which is such a shame as we had some lovely old buildings. All the walks have gone, much to my regret, I liked those very much. In the springtime it was very pleasant to smell the hawthorn bushes in the hedgerows and one year I remember the field, now Bush Field, was a complete carpet of yellow dandelions, not smart flowers but what a sight I never forgot. We had some lovely woods I used to play in, all gone now all dug out for clay and chalk, just big holes in ground that you cant replace. Some of the pits did get filled in behind the High Street, near the Grove, they turned them into a playing field and sports ground. Sometimes on a warm summer evening we would walk out to Newen Hill and out to the "Royal Oak", but like everything else has all gone! As well as Steeple Hill going towards Knockhall and the same at the lower end of Southfleet Road, there is no field now where we used have a yearly fair, we looked forward very much to it. Also at the riverside at Greenhithe we had a nice park with good views of the river and there were three training ships in those days

Ingress Abbey Gates and Park with HMS Worcester in background then HMS Warspite and HMS Arethusa

The shops are much the same, a few new ones, a few altered in appearance, and a few changed hands, but will still can obtain practically all we need locally. We still have our two Churches and Methodists Chapel and the Churches in the Greenhithe area, but there are a few minor chapels that have closed. I remember the fire that destroyed the Church after being struck by lighting. I remember taking part in a concert arranged by Harmer Road School to raise money for its restoration, and we were duly proud of our old church.

Well I don't know of many more things to comment on except, we all stuck together and helped each other, and all the houses were eventually repaired or replaced, and so we have progressed from a quite little village to quite a busy little town. We once had a Parish Council, we now have a Urban District Council and I may say over the years we have had much to thank all our councillors for. Quite Roads where all were safe and the children could play hop-scotch and whiptop, and bowl their hoops and skip to school. Instead we have all kinds of mechanical things up and down our streets like mad things, but that's progress we're told. But I wonder how an old man named Mr Perry would get his piggy on a string, tied its back legs, through the streets these days. He had styes in the fields by the walks and to meet a piggy coming down was my one terror. I did the mile in less than 4 minutes, and I didn't let the grass grow under my feet when I saw cows and pigs coming along. I wonder how many were the same as me. Well I cant think of anymore to write, so I hope I have recalled a few bits about Swanscombe in the past.

Mrs Stone (1972)

Watching the Football c1930

The above picture show's the men of Swanscombe watching Swanscombe United play a match in the 1930's. You may recognize some of the faces in this picture, my Grandfather Frederick Durling is sitting on the floor 5th from the left, he was a well known person in Swanscombe mainly due to having a wooden leg which he lost due to Osteoporosis a bone disease, you can see his wooden left leg sticking out on the grass. Apparently all the men would watch Swanscombe teams one week then walk down the footpath to watch Northfleet United the next

Footpath to Ebbsfleet 2011

Chapter 10

The War Years
World War 1 and World War 2

World War 1

World War I (**WWI**), which was predominantly called the **World War** or the **Great War** from its occurrence until 1939, and the **First World War** or World War I thereafter, was a major war centred in Europe that began on 28 July 1914 and lasted until 11 November 1918. It involved all the world's great powers, which were assembled in two opposing alliances: the Allies (centred around the Triple Entente) and the Central Powers (originally centred around the Triple Alliance). More than 70 million military personnel, including 60 million Europeans, were mobilised in one of the largest wars in history. More than 9 million combatants were killed, largely because of great technological advances in firepower without corresponding advances in mobility. It was the sixth deadliest conflict in world history.

The assassination on 28 June 1914 of Archduke Franz Ferdinand of Austria, the heir to the throne of Austria-Hungary, was the proximate trigger of the war. Long-term causes, such as imperialistic foreign policies of the great powers of Europe, including the German Empire, the Austro-Hungarian Empire, the Ottoman Empire, the Russian Empire, the British Empire, France, and Italy, played a major role. Ferdinand's assassination by a Yugoslav nationalist resulted in a Habsburg ultimatum against the Kingdom of Serbia. Several alliances formed over the past decades were invoked, so within weeks the major powers were at war; via their colonies, the conflict soon spread around the world.

On 28 July, the conflict opened with the Austro-Hungarian invasion of Serbia, followed by the German invasion of Belgium, Luxembourg and France; and a Russian attack against Germany. After the German march on Paris was brought to a halt, the Western Front settled into a static battle of attrition with a trench line that changed little until 1917. In the East, the Russian army successfully fought against the Austro-Hungarian forces but was forced back by the German army. Additional fronts opened after the Ottoman Empire joined the war in 1914, Italy and Bulgaria in 1915 and Romania in 1916. The Russian Empire collapsed in 1917, and Russia left the war after the October Revolution later that year. After a 1918 German offensive along the western front, United States forces entered the trenches and the Allies drove back the German armies in a series of successful offensives. Germany agreed to a cease-fire on 11 November 1918, later known as Armistice Day.

By the war's end, four major imperial powers—the German, Russian, Austro-Hungarian and Ottoman Empires—had been militarily and politically defeated and ceased to exist. The successor states of the former two lost a great amount of territory, while the latter two were dismantled entirely. The map of central Europe was redrawn into several smaller states. The League of Nations was formed in the hope of preventing another such conflict. The European nationalism spawned by the war and the breakup of empires, the repercussions of Germany's defeat and problems with the Treaty of Versailles are generally agreed to be factors in the beginning of World War II.

Swanscombe men went to war, as most of the men from around the empire joined up the call to arms. A huge government recruiting drive started, with posters and adverts put up everywhere.

Recruiting Posters

Black Soldiers, Milton Road, 1918. Negro American soldiers marching to work at the Swanscombe Cement Factory. Swanscombe Cement Works lost vast numbers of its workforce to the army and navy - these were replaced by women and by black American troops who loaded cement required by the American forces for the war effort. Until this time non-white faces were almost unknown and after 1918 the black Americans left. During the 1920s and 1930s an occasional Indian visited Swanscombe selling silks and other goods from a suitcase. It has only been since the 1970s that larger numbers of ethnic minorities have lived in Swanscombe.
(From Christoph Bull "Swanscombe in old picture postcards" 2005)

Handbook for all new recruits

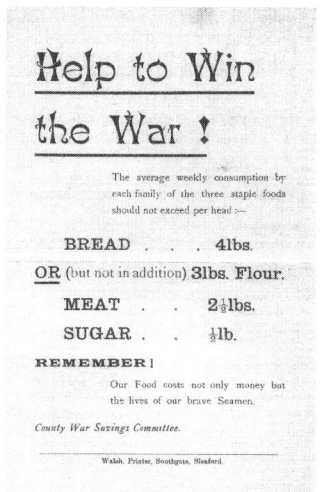

National ID Card 1915

Weekly allowance ration

Front page 11th November 1918

Women workers in the stave yard cement works 1914-1918

World War 1 Soilders

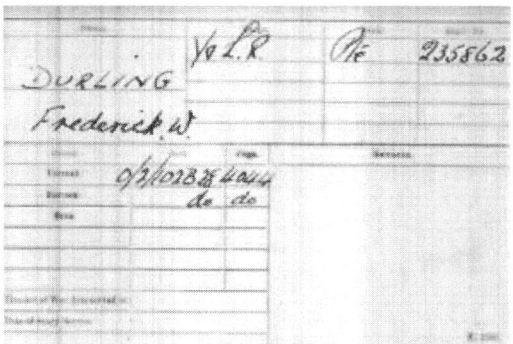

Above are the Recruitment Document, Photo of Frederick W Durling of 57 Church Road and the medal card

FORMER FOOTBALLER. — A member of the Swanscombe United football team in its hey-day, Mr. George Edward Durling, aged 56, of 36, Stanhope Road, died last week, after a short illness. He had been employed at White's Works for 40 years. During the war he served in the R.A.M.C. The funeral took place on Monday at Swanscombe Cemetery. The mourners were: The widow, Mr. F. Durling (son), Mrs. F. Gilbey (daughter), Mr. and Mrs. G. Stanley (son-in-law and daughter), Mr. W. Durling (brother), Mrs. J. Rixon, Mrs. N. and Mrs. W. Stanley Houghton (sisters), and Mrs. W. Stanley.

George Edward Durling my Great Grandfather in his WW1 RAMC Uniform
During the war he was gassed by mustard gas and in the end it killed him

Remembrance 1914-2014

In World War 1 the cost of Britain and the Commonwealth soldiers who lost their lives or were wounded was high, in total the British and Commonwealth troops were 908,000 killed and 2,123,000 wounded. To honour this sacrifice to those who died or were seriously injured it was decided to award the men of Swanscombe who had served their King & Country a medal of thanks. The Rvd Stanley Morgan and Cllr Ballard chose the medal to be awarded from a shortlist provided by Rvd Coleridge. This winning design, was manufactured by T Freeman in Birmingham and were hallmarked silver. Cllr Arthur Mercer was responsible for collating the names of those men eligible to receive the medal. The council paid £215 (about £9,400 now) for the medals. They were presented on the 1st November 1919 at Church House, Galley Hill. In addition, the medal was also presented to the families of all those who lost their lives serving King & Country during the Great War. My great aunt showed me two medals she had one for her father and one for her brother.

Information courtesy of Christoph Bull, Clive Wells & Bob Bareham. Image © Clive Wells 2013.

Arthur Edmund Aainsley, Arthur Arrows, John Anderson, James Austen, Archibald Stanley Aylward, Richard Baker, Percy Baker, Henry Barden, Leonard Bardoe, Cecil Bare, William Mosebury Bare, Walter Bareham, Leonard Barnes, Parcy Bartholomew, George C Berriman, Timothy Bignell, Frederick Birchley, Herbert Charles Bobby, John Bobby, Arthur Bodie, George Bodie, William Bolton, William Bones, Wilfred Stanley Thomas Bowen, Ernest Reginald Bridger, Samuel John Robert Bright, Edward Broad, Thomas Broad, Charles N Broad, Job Brown, John Busby, Robert A Butchard, Stanley Chandler, Richard Cornelius Cherry, Ernest Clark, Charles Clements, Percy Cole, George Albert Collins, Percy Cooper, Thomas R J Couchman, William Robert Croucher, George Crust, Harry Robert Dange, Henry Danzey, Elvey Arthur Day, John Henry Down, Henry J Dunmall, George A Edwards, James Charles Ellen, Fredrick George Ellen, Alfred Embleton, George Ewen, George Eyres, Alfred Victor Farmer, George Farmer, Henry George Farmer, Charles William Finch, Francis David Flint, Robert Flint, Harold James Foreman, Ernest Freeman, Russell W G Gatfield, Horace Leonard Gilbert, John Thomas Giles, Thomas Godden, Thomas Godden, Charles Thomas Godwin, Ernest Walter Graves, Henry Gray, Robert Green, Stephen R Groombridge, John Gurr, Walter Harding, Edward William Hardy, Albert James Harris, Edward Cyril Haylock, Charles Hazel, Arthur Hills, Joseph Hoadley, William Hoadley, Albert Edward Howard, Fredrick Hudson, Donald Humble, Percy Fredrick Jackson, Robert James, Thomas Jarvis, Harold Jessup, Edwin William King, Herbert George Kitchener, Reginald Larmer, Charles Edward Latter, Henry Thomas Loft, William Loft, Herbert Leonard Ernest Ludlow, Albert Luxford, Fredrick Malyon, William Thomas Malyon, James Vincent Mannering, Fred Martin, Hurbert Martin, Geoffrey William James Martin, George Mason, Charles Alfred Mason, William Maton, Francis Henry Medhurst, Stewart William Mercer, John William Messam, George Thomas Moss, Herbert Edwin Newdick, William Thomas Obee, Louis john Openshaw, Harry Outred, Harry Ovens, Charles William Palmer, John James Pearmain, Charles Pennell, Robert Thomas Perkins, John A Wynyard Peyton, Ernest Phillips, James Piper, William Plummer, Thomas Owen Poll, Fredrick Price, John Randle, William Henry Raven, Oscar H S Roberts, Henry Robinson, William Francis Robinson, Charles William Roots, Arthur Russell, John Russell, George Ernest Seaden, Henry Alfred Simmons, John Henry Simmons, Nelson Skews, Alfred Leonard Smith, Percy Edward Smith, Arthur South, Edwin B Stanley, Stanley S S Stedman, Louis Stevens, Alfred Richard Stone, Harry Stoneham, Harry George Street, William Sullivan, Alfred Tickner, Frederick Tickner, Alfred John Tigwell, John Tucker, George Turner, William Turner, George F Vine, Fred Wood Walker, Robert Duppa Walter, William Roger Walter, Harry Charles Weller, George Joseph White, John James White, Benjamin Wood, Arthur Woodger,

They shall grow not old, as we that are left grow old:
Age shall not weary them, nor the years condemn.
At the going down of the sun and in the morning,
We will remember them.

FOR MORE INFORMATION ON THE SWANSCOMBE SOILDERS AND MEMORIAL PLEASE VISIT
WWW.SWANSCOMBEMEMORIAL.CO.UK

World War 2

The modern world is still living with the consequences of **World War 2**, the most titanic conflict in history. On September 1st 1939, Germany invaded Poland without warning sparking the start of World War Two. By the evening of September 3rd, Britain and France were at war with Germany and within a week, Australia, New Zealand, Canada and South Africa had also joined the war. The world had been plunged into its second world war in 25 years. Six long and bloody years of total war, fought over many thousand of square kilometres followed. From the Hedgerows of Normandy to the streets of Stalingrad, the icy mountains of Norway to the sweltering deserts of Libya, the insect infested jungles of Burma to the coral reefed islands of the pacific. On land, sea and in the air, Poles fought Germans, Italians fought Americans and Japanese fought Australians in a conflict, which was finally settled with the use of nuclear weapons. World War 2 involved every major world power in a war for global domination and at its end, more than 60 million people had lost their lives and most of Europe and large parts of Asia lay in ruins.

As like in the previous war the men of Swanscombe went to war

No 16 ARP Wardens 1940 .Back Row 5th from Left George Lee. 8th Gerry Hicks. 11th Jack Parker, Womens ARP 1940

March past of Swanscombe Home Guard, Church Road, 3 December 1944. This is the 'B' company of the 17th Battalion of the Kent Home Guard, which covered Swanscombe. The Home Guard began in 1939 and was originally the Local Defence Volunteers, who only had two rifles between them. The Home Guard met at the Methodist Chapel in Church Road (later the Scouts Headquarters) but soon transferred to Galley Hill School on London Road for their headquarters. There were two patrols at night consisting of three men each (usually two older men and one young lad who was the runner of messages) that patrolled Swanscombe. Drilling, exercises and combat training also take place on the football ground within the Recreation Ground. The march past was a morale boost for all and taking the salute outside the fire station (later the library) are members of Swanscombe Urban District Council. This was the official stand down of the Swanscombe Home Guard. Note on the right the terraced houses with brick marks – this terrace was to have been extended until Swanscombe Parish Council purchased the land for the fire station in 1907. *(From Christoph Bull "Swanscombe in old picture postcards" 2005)*

ARP Amubulance 1940 Ambulance No 18 Mrs G.Liddey Extreme Left back row with Glasses. Mrs Tickner standing 5th from left Front Row.

The outbreak of war caused much disruption to everyday life of people in Swanscombe, such as food shortages, power cuts, and the fact that all the men were away, the women had to do all the work. But by far the worst was bomb damage and evacuation of the children.

There are many stories of evacuees, some had very happy times while being away and some like my father John Durling who was sent to Pangbourne in Reading with his sister Katherine, had a unpleasant time away.

Evacuees at Gravesend Pier and Station

Wartime Memories

By Peter Gear of Ames Road

I was playing with a group of friends where we lived when I was 6 years old when we heard a wailing noise. A man passing said, "You kids get home, this is an air raid." Not knowing what an air-raid was we ran. By this time there were lots of aeroplanes. It was frightening because there were so many and noisy. We had an Anderson Shelter in our garden to we all got into it. The windows had brown sticky paper as crosses on them so if they blew in it stopped flying glass. There was a black out where a crack of light was not to be seen, so some of us kids would go round some of the roads shouting "put that light out". We didn't have any bulbs in our bedrooms so light wasn't left on or show through cracks in the curtains. We went to school but classes were often disrupted several times a day and we spent a lot of time in the shelter. We were frightened every time the sirens went. The drone of the planes, the 'ack ack' of the guns, watching tracer bullets in the sky were all very scary. Sometimes I would look up during a raid to watch, the first planes we saw used to drop flares which had parachutes attached to them so the aircrew could see the ground, they also dropped incendiary bombs which would burst into flames upon contact with the ground. We were relieved when the all clear sounded. We grew up quickly but we lived from one air-raid to the next. It seemed never ending. Food was rationed which was difficult as we were always hungry, but all the people were in the same situation so we all helped each other. We had to carry our gas masks with us every where, hoping you never had to wear it. I was lucky as when children were being evacuated, my mother kept us at home. We played all the time in the fields in the pits and down at the disused trains. I remember the night the Morning Star was hit I was asleep when I heard the blast and the fire, then next morning I saw the what was left of the pub. The day when Broad Road was hit by a doddlebug I was talking with my mother in the garden, when we heard a whooshing sound we looked up and saw the doddlebug V1 gliding down, then all of a sudden swerved to the left and went down, we felt the blast and saw the black cloud of smoke and fire shoot into the air. One of our windows was blown out we were lucky others were not.

Photo of Bomb Damage taken by Len Todd 1944

By John Durling 28 Stanhope Road

By the time war broke out, I was 5 years old, so to us at that age war seemed like a big adventure, of course this seemed to fade when the food became rationed and bombs began to drop, and even worse we were sent away. I can remember mostly the end of the war, which filled with routine playing in the bomb sites swapping shrapnel which I used to keep in a large OXO tin. The most sought after pieces were the nose cone from a bomb or parts of shot down German planes, this was made difficult as all downed planes were cordoned off by the home guard or ARP. The only real outlet we had was the pictures which we went to twice a week, thanks mainly to my brother Richard (Dicky) who after he finished work in Gravesend would take me along. My father used to take me hunting with him and our dog roughchops who was a Labrador cross Cocker Spanial . We used to wait for the tied to come in then wait for the ducks to fly, my father would shoot them with his shotgun, then roughchops would go and pick the duck up. Then we would go rabbit hunting, we would find a rabbit run and snare it. Sometimes we would shoot them, after they were cooked we would spit the buckshot out into dishes. My father would also grow all our vegetables on his allotment, which he would sell in Swanscombe to make some money. Fruit we would scrump from orchards and wild fruit trees, berries we would collect and take home. This was the only way we could suppliment our diet, as I remember being always hungry.

When in September 1940 the Battle of Britain was in full swing I watched the dogfights in the sky it was brilliant, the noise of the spitfires hurricanes and 109's the smoke trails crisscrossing the sky. Then later when the Blitz started and the air-raid sirens going of every night this was scary as after a raid you did not know who would be alive the next day. We had an indoor Morrison shelter, which was approximately 6 feet 6 inches (2m) long, 4 feet (1.2m) wide and 2 feet 6 inches (0.75m) high. When not in use as a shelter it was used as a table. During the Blitz we had two near misses one was the Morning Star pub which was bombed as my dad only moments earlier left before it received a direct hit. I remember a lady who played the piano that night, she survived but used two sticks to walk about on. The other one was during a air-raid we heard a bang on the door, we remember saying who's that at the door, my dad got up and went to see who was there opened the door and found a foot long piece of shrapnel stuck in the door, where it came from we don't know but it went in my OXO tin. Night's were boring you could not go out due to blackout, we did have the radio to keep us informed, we had a pie with a sunset on the front. We had to take the battery to Mr Hodges shop, which is now Ladbrookes to get it charged.

Winter months were cold we had ice on the inside of the windows, coal was in short supply we used to collect it from the side of the railway however it never burnt as it was only supposed to be used in train boilers. During the Blitz we were advised that all children would be evacuated. We went to Gravesend station then to London then onto Pangbourne Reading, I don't remember to much about this time as I was only 6, but I went with my sister Kathleen (Peg) we stayed in a farmhouse with a family called Smith. When Mrs Smith went into the village we had to eat in the shed. The other thing is when their daughter played the piano, we had to stand and watch, this lasted about 2 months then we went home.

In 1943 my dad had some bad news, his Grandmother received a Navy telegram saying her son George Durling while serving in the Merchant Navy was torpedoed in the Mediterranean and was missing presumed dead, but as she read the telegram my uncle George walked up the path and into the kitchen, my Grandmother turned white and fainted. It turns out that he was in a lifeboat for two weeks and was picked up by a warship then sent back home. He was in WW1 and WW2

George Durling BEM WW1 & WW2 Medals

S.S.Otranto which was a troop carrier

In 1944 near the end of the war I remember when the V1 doddlebugs first came. My Dad and i were standing on the chicken shed watching a Doodlebug then the engine cut out! It seemed to be heading right for us, my dad yelled get mother in the shelter we ran in the house and all got in the Morrison shelter I was last in and as I got in I hit my head on the frame ouch!. Then we waited? The Doodlebug went up over Galley Hill Church then down into the lake next to the White Wharf Jetty and exploded. Phew.

V1 Doddlebug

V2 Rocket

There used to be an AK-AK Gun at the bottom of Stanhope, I used to go down and look at it all the time, and you could always hear firing during the air-raid tracer bullets like lasers in the night sky. One day I was standing in the kitchen doorway when an explosion blew me out of the doorway and onto the stove, I was glad the oven was not on. When I was at Manor Road School I was sitting in the classroom when I heard a whoosh sound a loud explosion, I looked out the window and saw a huge cloud rising up into the sky, it later turned out to be a V2. Also in 1944 the department of works opened a POW camp in Swanscombe I used to watch the German Soldiers through the fence, it was the first time I had seen a German. Later my Sister Kathleen fell in love and Married Richard Fuertig a German Czech army driver captured in 1944 France

We had VE Day party at school which was fun and VJ Party after that, after the war things took a long time to improve and when I joined the Merchant Navy in 1954 we still had rationing.

I went to school first at Harmer Road school which was next to our back garden, I then went to Manor Road School the headmaster was Charlie (Bawley) Grant, whom was also a councillor. I was the captain of the cricket team and was quite a good bowler at the time. My next school was Knockhall Road school and when I left I started as an apprentice cabinet maker at Wilsons which was in the old Galley Hill school in London Road.

 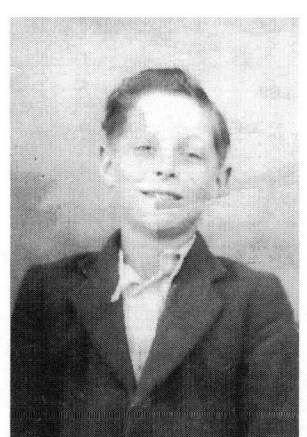 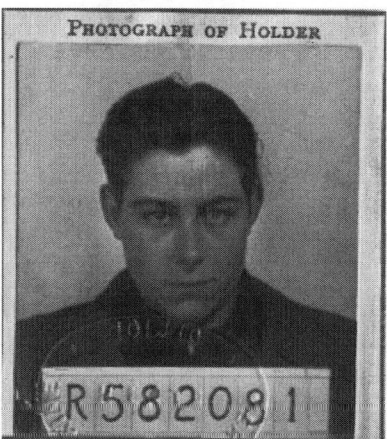

Frederick Durling holding George and Katherine in garden 28 Stanhope Road 1933, and John Durling taken at Manor Road School 1943 and Merchant Navy 1954

Bomb Damage

Trebble Road and Ames Road V1 Damage 1944

Bomb damage in Trebble Road and Ames Road. Another view of one of Swanscombe's many bombing incidents during the Second World War. The view shows Ames Road joining Trebble Road after a raid in early November 1944. Despite the damage only one person was killed with eight more in hospital and 21 needing first aid. The actual damage caused six houses to be totally destroyed with seven more having to be demolished. Some eighty people were sent to a rest centre and Swanscombe was very well organised in dealing with vast amounts of damage. This incident was caused by a VI flying bomb. *(From Christoph Bull "Swanscombe in old picture postcards" 2005)*

ARP wardens 1940

Ames and Lewis Road Bomb Damage 1943 2 Killed 48 Families Homeless 64 Homes Damaged

Bomb damage: Ames Road and Lewis Road. A photograph showing high explosive bomb damage, the bombs being dropped at 1.19 a.m. on, 18th May 1943. Raids such as this created huge logistical problems for Swanscombe Urban District Council, in rehousing families and clearing debris to make roads passable. The houses shown here were model dwellings built by the council: Ames Road in the late 1920s and Lewis Road in the 1930s. Apparently two small boys were blown onto a roof by the blast suffering only minor injuries. *(From Christoph Bull "Swanscombe in old picture postcards" 2005)*

Broad Road Bomb Damage 1944 by Len Todd

Broad Road Bomb Damage 7th August 1944 V1 Doodlebug by Len Todd

Air-raid damage. Broad Road. This view is of the damage caused on 7 August 1944 when a V1 (flying bomb) destroyed four houses because it fell short of its intended destination of London. The emergency services and Swanscombe Urban District Council then had to re-house 48 families, treating the injured and making the area safe from collapsing buildings and any unexploded bombs. The photograph shows how the ground floor of the houses was filled with the rubble from the bedrooms and roof and also the Victorian iron fireplaces, which were rarely used to heat the bedrooms because of the cost of fuel. *(*From Christoph Bull "Swanscombe in old picture postcards" 2005)

Another view Broad Road 1944 by Len Todd

Ministry of Works Swanscombe POW Camp 154

After the Allied invasion of western Europe took place in 1944 prisoners that were taken would be transported on large barges (along with wounded Allied troops) over the English Channel and would dock at a major ports such as Southampton and Portsmouth. Sometimes discipline would break down and officers would be jostled and abused by enlisted men although in general this was not the case. Here they would be deloused and board trains which would take them to one of the nine Command Cages which would be set up in racecourses such as Kempton Park Doncaster Catterick and Loughborough in Leicestershire or football grounds such as Preston North End's ground in Lancashire, Northern England. A cage was a place where PoWs would be held before being sent to a PoW camp and during their stay there they would be interrogated by the Prisoner of War Interrogation Section (PWIS) under the command of Lieutenant A.P. Scotland who's main base was in No. 8 Kensington Palace Gardens which was a former stately home. It was near here, in Cockfosters, that prisoners who were thought to have vital information as well as Luftwaffe flying crews were sent for special interrogation. Interrogation methods were very thorough and employed various means to extract information from prisoners. One such method was to "plant" an undercover soldier who spoke fluent German (usually a Pole who joined forces with the British) to glean as much information as possible from other prisoners. At around this time after the interrogation process was done the PoWs would then be sent around the country to the 600 camps which, had by this time been or being built

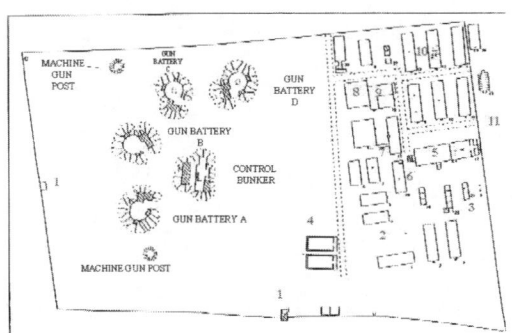 

Plan of a typical POW camp in England   Typical scene for people in 1944 as POW were taken to their camps

Swanscombes PoW camp 154 was built on a field in Swanscombe Street. The main entrance was opposite the Blue Anchor Pub, the camp was surround by wire fence with barbed wire around the top. The camp was on the site were Keary Road is today. On the most part the German PoWs were very friendly and polite, and did not cause much trouble. Some of the women used to work in the camp either as cooks or cleaners, which led to girls falling in love with some of them and later after the war when the camp closed some getting married, like my Aunt Katherine (Peg) did.

Every Sunday the PoWs were allowed to go church, and we would watch them marching past up the High Street. The camp closed in 1948 and was later used by people to live in while the houses and prefabs were being constructed

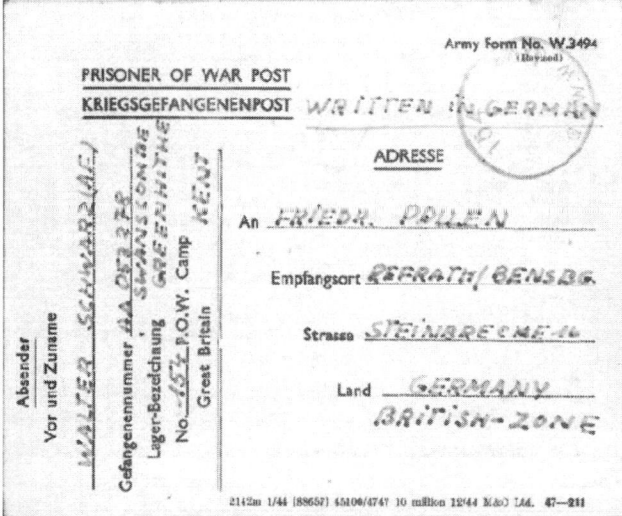

PoWs Postcard sent home 1946

War Memorial's

THESE ALL GAVE THEIR LIVES 1914-1918
JOHN ANDERSON : RICHARD BAKER : PERCY BARDEN
HENRY BARDEN : LEONARD BARDOE : CYRIL BARE
WILLIAM BARE : WALTER BAREHAM : GEORGE C BERRIMAN
JOHN BOBBY : HERBERT C BOBBY : WILLIAM BONES
WILFRED S BOWEN : SAMVEL BRIGHT : EDWARD BROAD
THOMAS BROAD : CHARLES N BROAD : ROBERT A BVTCHARD
ERNEST CLARK : GEORGE CRVST : HENRY DALTRY
HENRY J DVNMALL : FRED G ELLEN : CHARLES W FINCH
ROBERT FLINT : HAROLD FOREMAN : THOMAS GODDEN
HENRY GRAY : ROBERT GREEN : STEPHEN R GROOMBRIDGE
JOHN GVRR : FRED HVDSON : THOMAS JARVIS
HAROLD JESSVP : WILLIAM LOFT : HVBERT MARTIN
STEWART W MERCER : HERBERT E NEWDICK : HARRY OVENS
JAMES J PIPER : WILLIAM PLVMMER : OWEN E POLL
FRED PRICE : HENRY ROBINSON : FRANK ROBINSON
GEORGE SEADEN : NELSON SKEWS : PERCY SMITH
ALFRED SMITH : LOVIS STEVENS : HARRY STONEHAM
WILLIAM SVLLIVAN : JOHN TVCKER : GEORGE TVRNER
WILLIAM TVRNER : GEORGE WEBSTER : HARRY WELLAR
GEORGE WHITE : JOHN WHITE : ARTHVR WOODGER
GLORY TO GOD WHO GAVE STRENGTH TO ENDVRE

Chapter 10

School's & Education

Galley Hill School

Galley Hill looking east, circa 1910. A view towards Northfleet with the George & Dragon public house on the furthest distance on the right. The terraced houses on the right dated from the 1850s and the vicarage for All Saint's Church was in the middle of this row. A large chalk pit just beyond the houses and the North Kent railway line behind severely restricted the space for housing. On the left is Galley Hill School, built in 1858, which by 1913 could hold over six hundred children and which served the needs of the expanding cement factory population. Beyond on the left was the original 1882 iron All Saint's Church, later used as a church house and social club (called the 17th club, so named after Swanscombe's Home Guard Battalion). Virtually every building in this picture had been demolished by 1986. *(*From Christoph Bull "Swanscombe in old picture postcards" 2005)

View of the same site taken in 2011

View of the old school while being demolished in 1986

Galley Hill School Photographs

This Photograph is a Durling family collection of Children at Galley Hill School taken around 1885

Class Photograph 1910

Class Photograph Christmas 1910

Class Photograph 1919

Class Photograph Christmas 1901 Donated by H Jarman

Manor Road Schools

The site where Manor Road School was to be built was once part of Swanscombe Wood and like most of that area was to undergo extensive building and regeneration once the cement works was built and consequently extended to over the years. Swanscombe Street was once the High Street and it was only natural that a school was built in that area as most of the population still lived there. So in 1877 it was decided another school was needed due to the ever growing population, as Galley Hill School was becoming to small to cope with demand.

Drawing of Manor Road School by Eileen Munns

The Schools were known by many names from 1877 to when it closed and moved in August 2008

Years:	Known as:	Headteachers:
1877 - 1902	Swanscombe National School for Boys	Christopher Peters
1902 - 1950	Swanscombe Church of England Boys	Charlie Grant
1951 – 1993	Swanscombe County Infant School	Margaret Wilson/Barr (1954-1980)
		Mrs. Pat Bassant (1980-1992)
		Mrs. Susan Harris (1992-1993)

They then moved to Keary Road from 1993 to when it closed in 2008.

April 1993	Swanscombe Infant School and Nursery moves to the former site of Swanscombe High School	
Sept 2004	Nursery School is opened	
August 2008	Swanscombe Infants School and Nursery	Mrs. Susan Harris (1993-2007)
		Mr David Lloyd (2007-2008)

The site now are houses, the only reference to the School are the street names, which are in honor of two former head teachers Mrs Barr & Mrs Bassant

Manor Road Primary School

Manor Road School 1986   Pupils with their mugs 1993

With the growth of Swanscombe increasing year on year with all the industry, which had been established, the Schools at Galley Hill and Eynesford Road were becoming filled up with workers children. So in 1877 a new school was planned and built, It was originally named as Swanscombe National School for Boys. In 1902 the school was renamed Swanscombe Church of England Boys School, but was known locally as Manor Road School. Then in 1951 it was renamed again to Swanscombe Infant School until its closure in 1993. The students were relocated to Sweyne Junior School. In 1993 when the school closed a unique commemorative mug was made to mark the closure of the school the headteacher at the time Susan Harris said funds from the sale would pay for new books. The former headmaster Charlie Grant was a former councilor and was also former football referee and keen cricketer.

Article in the Dartford Times 6th February 1997

Former pupils of Manor Road Primary School, are being urgently sought by the Housing Association. The old flint built school is due to be demolished to make way for 14 new three bedroom houses on the site. The old flints which made up the bulk of the old building will be used in the restoration of St Peter & Paul Church. They would like any former pupil at the school who is interested in living in the houses to contact the association for consideration.

Site of the old Manor Road School now named after the old Headmistress Mrs Barr 2011

Manor Road School Photographs

Manor Road School Photograph 1959 from Durling Collection
Alan Aspinal John Stoneham Georgette Wilsher Joan Hopper Sally Gibb Ronald Palmer Stephen Arthur
Angela Errington Anthony Fry Jean Hartfield Keith Stilwell Patricia Durling Mary Lingham Freddy Russell
Merren Woolton Colin Raymond Pauline Short Roy Marsh David Saunders Trevor Parish

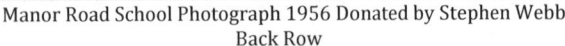

Manor Road School Photograph 1956 Donated by Stephen Webb   Back: Mrs Wingfield Teacher? Mrs Hopkins
Back Row   Mrs Margaret Barr (Wilson)
Derek Stevens Stephen Webb Stuart Titsel Malcolm Collier Malcolm Alright
Sally Gibbs Paul Long Niel Butcher Carol Blackwell Mrs Margaret Barr (Wilson)
Middle Row
Margaret Venus Susan Young Linda Bobby Alan Mitchell Christopher Hopkins
Alec Barnes Kenny Herbert Roy Marsh Peter Bobby
Front Row
Ernie Walton Christopher Barham Robert Cloke Roy Finnis Lynn Edgley
Brian Francis Stephen Churcher Sandra Collins Glynis May

Manor Road Community Primary School

SWANSCOMBE: New primary school to celebrate opening
By Abigail Foulkes »

A SWANSCOMBE primary school is to mark the official opening of its new building.

Manor Road Under Construction

Headteacher Gavin Evans outside the school

Manor Community Primary School in Keary Road was born out of a merge between Swanscombe Infant School in Swanscombe Street and Sweyne Junior School in Keary Road two years ago.

Sweyne Junior School was demolished and pupils and staff moved over to temporary units on the other site.

But on November 25, the pupils will set off balloons and celebrate the completion of their brand new building in Keary Road, before staff hold a formal ceremony to mark the official opening.

Headteacher Gavin Evans said: "It has been a long two years but it has been well worth the wait.

"Pupils, staff, parents and governors have all been absolutely amazed at the finished article and I can't wait to see the impact it has on our standards of education."

It was decided the two schools should merge as a decreasing birth rate in the area meant both schools had spare capacity. But no jobs have been lost in the merge.

The Department for Education and Kent County Council poured £7.2million into the new school in 2008, which saw the creation of a 250-seater theatre for performing arts and a dance studio.

Executive headteacher David Lloyd said: "This new building is a huge boost to the work of the school in the community.

"We hope it will help give our children and families a community asset of which we can all be proud and will help and inspire everyone to be the best that we can."

Article in the News Shopper 23rd November 2010

Harmer Road School

Harmer Road School 1998

Harmer Road School was built in 1898 just off Stanhope Road. The school had two classrooms and a reception room on the side. There were two entrances on either end. Out the back was a large playground area, in the 1970's the school was converted into a youth club where the young of Swanscombe could spend time in the evening. In 2007 the old building was knocked down to make way for flats.

Harmer Road Flats 2011

Harmer Road School Photograph 1955 donated by B McMillian

Harmer Road Reception class 1952

George James Durling died aged 6

Southfleet Road School & Sweyne Junior School

Southfleet Road Community School opened in 1939 and operated as an infants and a junior and secondary school. One part of the school was the infant and junior school, which accommodated primary aged boys and girls from 5 years old to 11 years old. The other part of the school was used as a secondary school for girls only aged 11 years old to 15 years old. The went of to either next door to Swanscombe Secondary School or various other schools in the area depending on where you lived. This continued like this until, on the 16th February 1971 Sweyne Junior School opened offering a junior school for girls and boys between 7 years old and 11 years old. The Sweyne was the main feeder school for Swanscombe Comprehensive and now Swan Valley Community School. The uniforms from Southfleet Road Primary was a navy gymslip with an acorn leaf logo and a red sash around the waist worn with a white blouse, in the 1950's and 60' a beret was also part of the uniform and the headmistress at the time was quite strict about the uniform worn outside of school because if you were caught not wearing your beret you would be strongly told off. By the late 1970's the uniform colour had changed to a deep red almost burgundy. The badge logo was a Viking ship similar to the one the council use.

Sweyne Junior School 1998

Southfleet Road Primary & Secondary School Photographs

School Photographs form the 1960s

Sweyne Junior School old badge

Southfleet Road Primary 1955

Southfleet Road Girls Secondary 1958

Mr Lawrence Mrs Karana Mrs Dreher Mr Beaty Mr Mortlock

Southfleet Road Girls Secondary 1958

Site of the old Sweynes & Southfleet Road Secondary & Primary 2011

Jean Durling School Photo age 7

Swanscombe Secondary School

Swanscombe Secondary School, Southfleet Road. The school had a very colourful history. It began in 1938 as a junior girls and infants in temporary buildings behind terraced houses in Southfleet Road. The site was originally part of the Mansion House estate and included orchards and a hop garden of same 15 acres. During the Second World War the new building was not used as a school because the huge glass windows were considered too dangerous if broken in air raids. After 1945 the school was extended and enlarged - it became the Swanscombe Secondary School for both sexes by 1967 and continued until 1992, when it was decided to close the school, demolish the buildings and scatter Swanscombe's considerable secondary school aged pupils to surrounding areas. The stupidity of this political move was clearly demonstrated when a new secondary school was then built on the site in 1998 being the first in the area for twenty years. The new school was called 'Swan Valley Community School' and was constructed under the controversial 'Private Finance Initiative' system of funding - the results of which future generations will inherit. In November 2002 Swanscombe's old branch library in Church Road closed and moved to a new accommodation within this new complex.
(From Christoph Bull "Swanscombe in old picture postcards" 2005)

The Heartbreak of the Final Lesson 1990

Dartford Reporter news report in 1990 on the closure of Swanscombe School

When the last teachers and pupils left Swanscombe School it was with lumps in their throats. After three years of fighting, campaigning and pleading, the school in Swanscombe Street closed last week. The once bustling buildings will not be filled with children in September and contractors will move in to convert the science block into classrooms for the nearby infants school in Manor Road. Chairman of Governors John Cherry said: "It was a very emotional day. "The pupils left at lunchtime and it was awful. Normally the last day of the summer term is nice but this was terrible. "We all had lumps in our throats." Headteacher Ron Halford has taken early retirement and all but two of the rest of the teachers have found new jobs. Following Swanscombe tradition, art teacher Ian Probert made all of the staff a leaving gift. In the past he has sketched any leaving teacher but this time he produced oil paintings of everyone. Mr Cherry said: "It was a touching thing to do and everyone was thrilled. Normally he would make a huge card that we all sign but these oil pictures were something extra special. "We all felt so disappointed after such a long hard battle. "The only consolation is that part of the buildings will be used by the infants school. The rest seems doomed for demolition which is a terrible shame." KCC first put a question mark over the school's future three years ago when it, Southfields School in Singlewell Road, Gravesend and Meopham School, Wrotham Road, were put under review. Numbers at Southfields went up, Meopham was awarded Grant Maintained Status and Swanscombe was closed down.

Swanscombe Secondary School

Swanscombe Central School Eynsford Road

Article in the Chronicle 4th May 1928

The ceremonial opening of Swanscombe Central School took place on Friday . The Rev S Morgan (chairman of the managers) presided, and there were also present Sir Mark Collet, Mr E Salter Davies (County Director of Education), Mr F W Gill, J P Alderman J Lawrence Mitchell and Mrs Mitchell, the Rev E F Campbell, Mr & Mrs W D Borland, Dr and Mrs Stanley, Mr Everard Hesketh, the Rev Canon and Mrs Gedge, the Rev and Mrs L Dudley Brown, the Rev E M Allen, Councillors, Miss Hewitt, Messrs E Moore, T W Ostle, J T Kemsley, F Lund, W J Bevis, Walter Ames, W E Gasson, W Townsend, A Entwistle, Miss E J Wigan, Mr A C Davis, the Rev Canon mad Mrs H T Powell, the Rev E A W Topley, Mr Hugh MacNaughton, M.A. (vice provost of Eton College), Mr C H Wells, Mrs Wheatley, Mr and Mrs Beaumont, Mr C Harrison, and Mr Laidler, The Proceedings opened with the singing of a hymn by the scholars and prayer by the Rev E F Campbell Ward, Rector of Swanscombe.

The reason the school was built was due to the fact that there was a need for an extra 300 spaces.
It was felt at the time less expensive building a new school than adding parts to existing schools in the area.

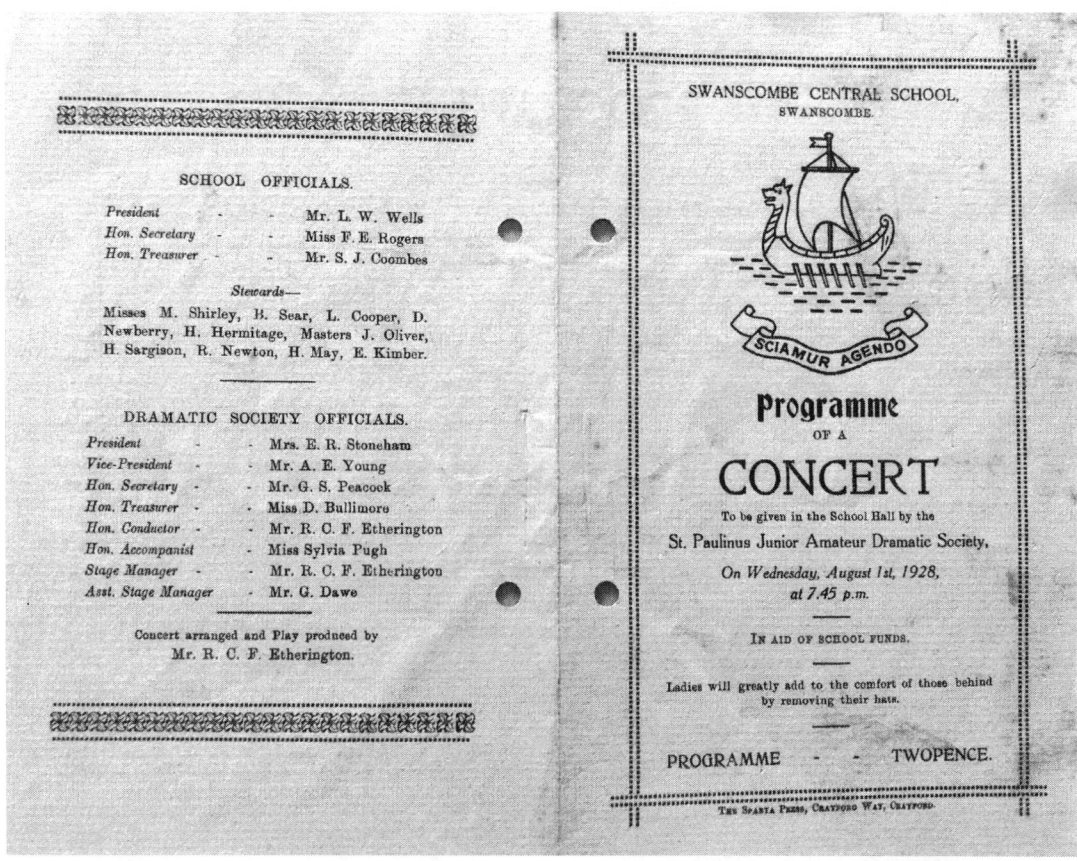

Concert Programme 1st August 1928

Swanscombe Central School Photograph 1954

Swanscombe Central School Building now Knockhall

Swanscombe Knockhall Council School Knockhall Road

The old Knockhall Road Primary School is no longer there today the site is now houses and a community centre

Knockhall School Badge   Sir Francis Belsey   Centenery Mosaic

The school was formally opened, on the 23rd August 1911, by Sir Francis Belsey, on behalf of the Kent Education Committee. The official name given to the school was "Swanscombe Knockhall Council School". It opened for the first intake of children on the 1st September 1911 and was attended by 90 boys and 100 girls taken from the Swanscombe and Greenhite areas. The first appointed headmaster was Alfred Tupman, he was in the post for thirty years. In 1952 the school was renamed to "Knockhall County Primary School". By the 1970's the old school building was becoming overcrowded and was starting to look its age and in area's in very poor condition. Swanscombe Central School at this time decided to move its pupils to secondary schools in Swanscombe and in Greenhite, and so the Primary School took over the building which was built in 1928.

Photograph of the old school taken in the 1970's

Swan Valley Community School

The residents of Swanscombe had to wait nearly seven years for the new school to be built, even then that was only the first phase. The school opened officially in September 1997. The first Principle was Mr K S Ogg. The School's catchment area was Swanscombe, Greenhihe and Stone and was the first secondary school to be built in Kent for over 25 years and could provide education for up to 900 pupils, or 180 pupils per year, plus a Sixth Form.

Two views of the School taken in 2012

The building was constructed to make use of all the natural light and space to best promote a positive learning experience. Classrooms are large and provide all the modern learning resources. Outside there are extensive and safe playing areas, with seats for students to enjoy fair weather. Phase two and the final wing of the building opened in 2002.

The old sign for Swan Valley which has since now changed to Ebbsfleet Valley.

As with most things in Swanscombe, the schools often change their name and so in 2013 Swan Valley Community School changes it name to Ebbsfleet Academy.

Swan Vally Tusk

During construction work at Swan Valley Community School in Kent a tusk belonging to an extinct species of elephant was unearthed. The village of Swanscombe has been a famous archaeological site since the early 20th Century when remains of "Swanscombe Man" were found, dated to about 400,000 years old - the second oldest human remains ever discovered in the UK. The tusk was partially excavated and identified by University of Southampton archaeologists Dr Francis Wenban-Smith and Dr Gilbert Marshall as belonging to a species called **Palaeoloxodon antiquus**, more commonly known as the straight-tusked elephant. This beast would have been about four metres tall and weighed about nine tons - much larger than a modern African or Asian elephant today. The school governors decided that this tusk big tusk should be dug up and put on display in the school along with several flint hand-axes found nearby.

They called upon the services of *Fieldworklogistics.com*, who carefully excavated the very fragile 1.5 metre-long tusk, created a rigid plaster jacket around the tusk, re-enforced with steel beams, and lifted it from the ground to carry it away on a purpose built stretcher.

The tusk was then brought to the professional conservators at **Natural-History-Conservation.com**. The field jacket was carefully removed only after the jacket and its contents had been allowed to dry out very slowly. The coarse gravel sediment was carefully cleaned away, and the very fragile and friable tusk was consolidated with a thin solution of a stable, reversible, adhesive. As the tusk is very weak and fragile, with literally thousands of fractures created by the constantly fluctuating conditions of alternate wet and dry periods experienced in river gravel sediments, a permanent rigid support was created for the tusk to lie on, perfectly fitting the contours of its underside.

Tusk on display in Swanscmbe Library

The tusk will soon be on display in the school along with the hand-axes and a large portrait and clay sculpture - made by the artists and modelmakers at *Modelspecimens.com* - recreating the extinct giant who roamed the area of Swanscombe some 400,000 years ago.

  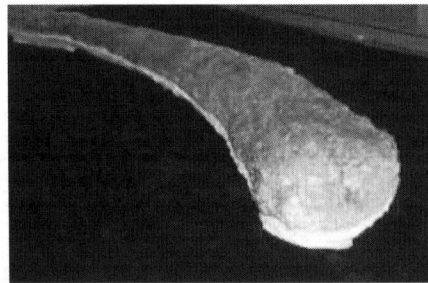

Excavation of the Tusk

Chapter 12

Football

Swanscombe Football

Association Football arrived in Swanscombe in 1890 when the men of the village created Swanscombe United, as like most of the country working hours were decreased so leisure time increased. The main sport at the time was cricket, which was played in the summer, and football was played in the winter months, much like today. In 1890 most of the current clubs we see today in the premiership were either amature or semi professional, Swanscombe was the latter and stayed that way until it finished a few years ago.

Swanscombe United 1909-1910

Although the above picture says 1909-10 this picture was taken in 1914 just before the war I can only assume this picture was taken then as the team was split up and went off to war. I know this because the man in front of the board is George Edward Durling. The board shows the period when Swanscombe were most successful, when they played in the Dartford District league. They played in Black Shorts with Red and Black striped shirts.

Dartford & District League Medal 1910, and another picture taken in 1914
Dartford & District League Winners 1908-1909
Dartford & District League Winners 1909-1910
Gravesend Borough League Winners 1909-1910

Swanscombe Athletic 1903-04

Swanscombe Athletic Football Club. 1903-1904. Working hours were still very long compared to today, some 54 hours a week for a cement worker in 1903 - but there was a gradual increase in leisure time. Consequently various organisations grew up such as sports clubs. political parties. cultural organisations and horticultural/livestock societies. The famous Swanscombe United Football Club with their red and black strip was the senior team, but Swanscombe Invicta was a rival. The team shown here was a break away from Invicta who, in 1903, became Swanscombe Athletic and probably shared the ground on the Rectory Field with the parent club. Swanscombe Athletic described itself as 'medium strength team. average age 19, with private ground and dressing room' in 1904, and could attract large crowds to matches: 1.000 watched a Swanscombe Invicta match in April 1904. Mr. Braine, the secretary on the picture, lived in Railway Street, Northfleet. Rivals Swanscombe United had their home pitch on land to the west of the cemetery and after 1932 the whole playing area was upgraded as part of the Recreation Ground. Swanscombe Athletic, like rivals United, does not exist today. *(From Christoph Bull "Swanscombe in old picture postcards" 2005)*

Other Teams

Swanscombe Reserves 1920-21 and Swanscombe Scouts FC 1924

Chapter 13

Adverts

This section of the book is a look back at some old Adverts that would have appeared in parish magazines and other publications in the past. Some of the names mentioned in this book so far also had their own adverts.

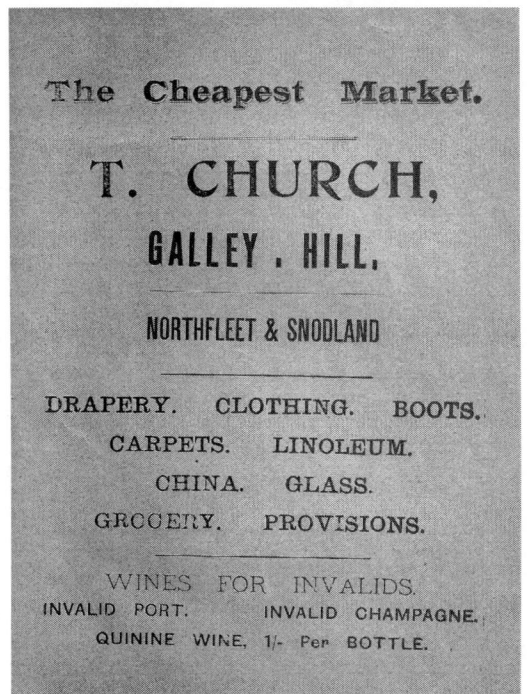

Parish Church Magazine May 1913

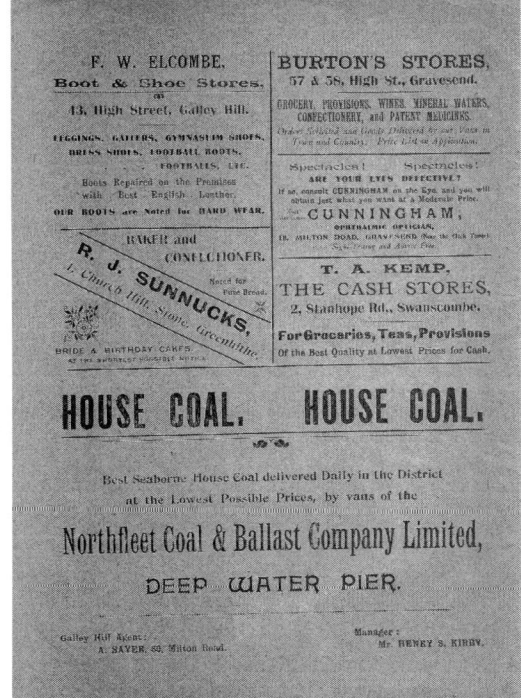
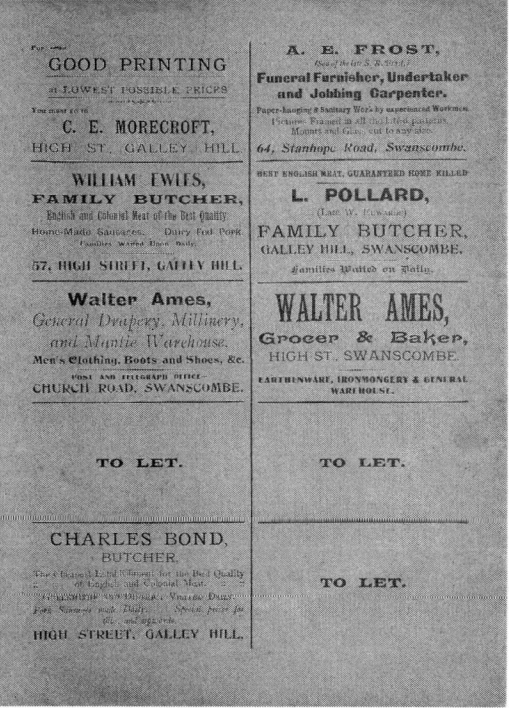

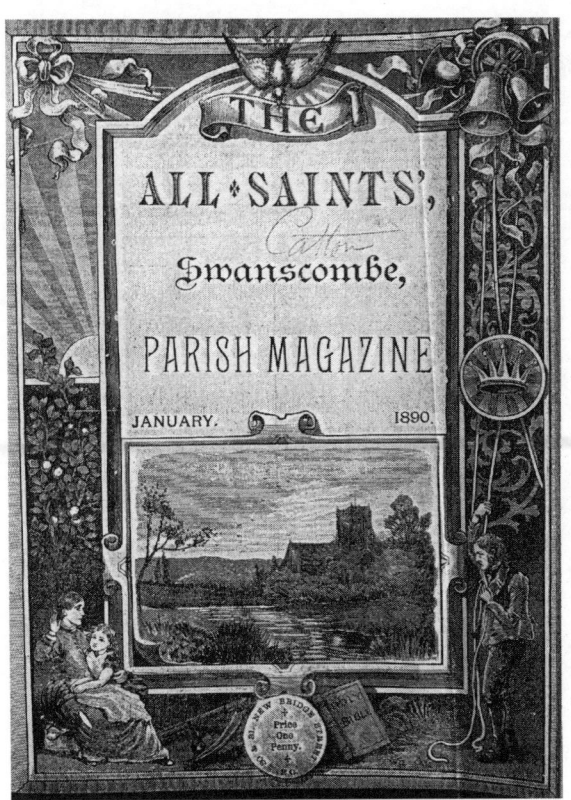

Parish Magazine 1890

Adverts 1960

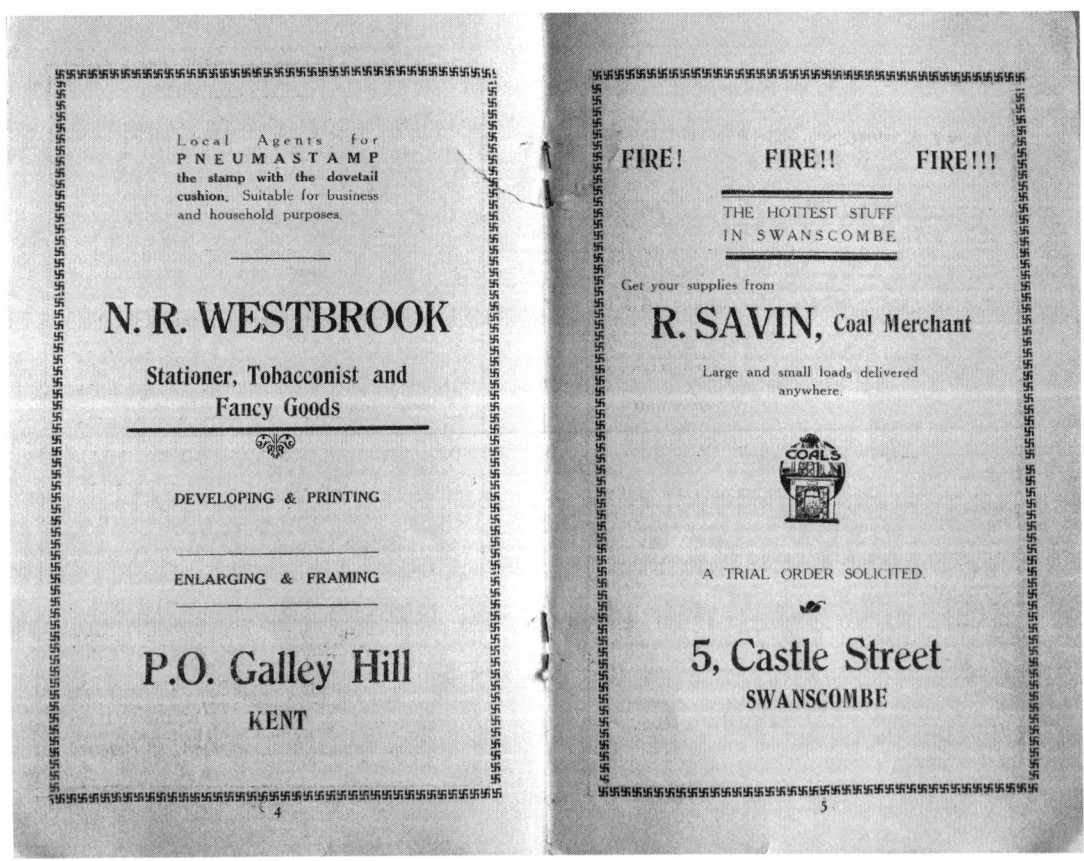

Advert 1931

MOORES' MINERAL WATERS

Famous since 1879

Moore Bros, (Swanscombe) Ltd,   Swanscombe

J. H. LINCOLN, M.P.S.
Dispensing Chemist

84, High Street, and 5, Dover Road
NORTHFLEET
Phone: Gravesend 755

Accurate Dispensing with Pure Drugs

National Health Service Dispensing

Phone: GRAVESEND 891.

L. THOMPSON,
FAMILY BUTCHER
ESTABLISHED 1908

Castle Street & Milton Street
Swanscombe.

Prime Ox Beef.   Canterbury Lamb and Mutton. -:- Dairy Fed Pork.
Families waited upon daily for orders.

G. H. MAY,
: **Family Butcher,** :
Church Road, Swanscombe.

Finest Chilled Beef and
Canterbury Lamb
Home Made Sausages.
FAMILIES WAITED UPON DAILY.

● **MORECROFT**
for
● **PRINTING** . .

70a, HIGH STREET
GALLEY HILL . .
Phone: GRAVESEND 1863

L. WARREN & J. BRIAN

RADIO AND ELECTRICAL
ENGINEERS

"HANDYMAN" REPAIR SERVICE

108, Swanscombe Street,
Swanscombe

Phone, Gravesend 4629

Swanscombe Car Hire Service

SERVICE DAY AND NIGHT

Booking Office:

1, Milton Road, Swanscombe, Kent

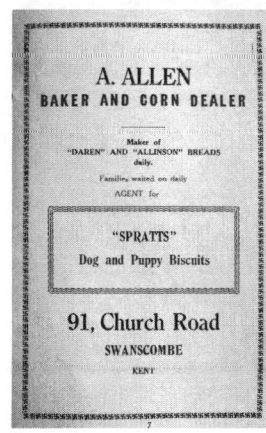

Adverts 1931   Adverts 1960

'Phone: GRAVESEND 4374

SWANSCOMBE POST OFFICE GRAVESEND 4375

AMES' STORES

CENTRAL SUPPLY
90-98 CHURCH ROAD, SWANSCOMBE

Departments: GROCERY, PROVISIONS (BACON SPECIALISTS),
Hardware, China, Glass & Earthenware

The Noted WOOL Shop for Botany, Cashmere Wools and all reliable Brands, Working and Instruction Leaflets
Stationery   Greeting Cards

LADIES AND GENTLEMEN'S   FANCY DRAPERY   HABERDASHERY   HOUSEHOLD GOODS & CURTAININGS
TAILORING AND OUTFITTING   GOWNS   CHILDREN'S WEAR   FOOTWEAR   GIFT ARTICLES

When post-war conditions permit, all departments will be fully stocked again with reliable and
best brands of goods at economy prices

COPYRIGHT

A. T. HUMPHREY,
39, Church Road.

Boot and Shoe Repairs
Workmanship Guaranteed.

Leather, Cut Soles, Rubbers, Rivets, Protectors, Polishes, Etc., Etc.

C. STEED

Greengrocer and Fruiterer

10a, Milton Street, Swanscombe

SUPPLIES FRESH DAILY

D. T. WILLIAMS,
M.P.S.,

Medical Hall, Swanscombe.

HIGH CLASS CHEMIST

Pure Drugs

Toilet Specialities

TRUSSES, BODY BELTS and ELASTIC STOCKINGS expertly fitted and supplied through your Friendly Society.

OPTICAL REPAIRS of all kinds a Speciality

'Phone: GRAVESEND 586.

WARD   for Wreaths, Crosses

and other designs artistically made of the
Choicest Flowers in Season

2, Windmill Street, Gravesend   'Phone 587
(next to Plaza Cinema)

WEDDING AND PRESENTATION BOUQUETS A SPECIALITY

Advert 1940

Chapter 14

**Airiel Photographs
&
Future Developments**

View's From Above

Two views taken from the stack at the Swnscombe Cement Works 1961 by Len Todd

Ariel view taken in 2009

When you compare this photograph from the photographs taken by Len Todd in 1961 you can see how Swanscombe has changed over the years. First thing you notice, are the "White Works" and the "Imperial Paper Mills", the railways tracks from the quarry's have all gone, the new housing in Swanscombe and the sports ground at the grove has been built, were previously a freshly filled chalk pit was. The new high speed line has been built with the new Ebbsfleet International Station just out of shot on the right. The Riverside at Northfleet has changed as well with new buildings at Tower Wharf "Seacon", no change with the football ground, but the main change since this was taken, the "Lefarge Northfleet Cement Works" has all but been demolished.

Future Development

Over the next decade Swanscombe will undergo a massive change as the borders between Ebbsfleet Valley and Northfleet merge ever closer and the green spaces will be replaced with a mulitude of houses and theme park that will soon be built.

Four new villages will be created as part of the Ebbsfleet scheme and the homes will be built across the Eastern Quarry next to Bluewater just off Southfleet Road, Ebbsfleet Station and the \Swanscombe peninsula.

In 2012, Hollywood film giant Paramount unveiled the £2 billion proposals to build one of Europe's largest theme parks in Swanscombe. The plans are designed by Tony Sefton.

The theme park will create approx 27,000 jobs, the 872-acre development planned is bigger than the Olympic Park.

The development will be a Paramount-branded entertainment resort, boasting attractions including Europe's largest indoor water park. Which will include theatres, live music venues, cinemas, restaurants. Hotels are also planned to open in just six years time on the currently derelict brownfield site.

The government is going to invest £200m to support 15,000 new homes and create the first Garden City for almost 100 years in Ebbsfleet Kent."

The concept of garden cities was developed by the liberal social reformer Sir Ebenezer Howard. In his book "Tomorrow: A Peaceful Path to Real Reform", published in 1898, he proposed cities of 30,000 people that were self-sufficient and ringed by an agricultural belt. Garden cities were a response to overcrowding and squalid living conditions in cities following the industrial revolution. They were intended to combine the best of urban life with access to nature.

So over the next 10-20 years the landscape of Southfleet Road and the Ebbsfleet Valley will change beyond all recognition.

We have now come to end of our story and I hope you have enjoyed looking back at how things were and are now and the things that are yet to come.

Like most families that still live or have lived in Swanscombe they will discover if they trace their ancestors back far enough, you will find that they moved to the area either before or just after the cement works started. My family moved from Ash around 1810 to live in "Stone" in the agricultural industry (Groom). The first member of the family to work at the cement works was Alfred in 1871 thereafter the chain was unbroken until my father decided to follow his uncle in the Merchant Navy in 1954.

To my Dad for always being there when we needed him the most

Written and Prouduced by

Mason Durling

&

Christoph Bull

© 2014

All items are available in Dartford Reference Library and many in Gravesend Reference Library.

BADDELEY, G E (ed) The Tramways of Kent by Invicta. Vol 1. 1971

BAKER, G Politics, Pollution and the Industrial Development of a North Kent Parish: Swanscombe 1840 - 1910. 1990

BOREHAM, P W The Stopes Family at Swanscombe (essay)

BULL, C R A concise history of Swanscombe, 1993, 1996, 2003

BULL, C R The Civil War and the Restoration in Gravesham 1642-1662. 1985

BULL, C R Northfleet in Old Picture Postcards. 1987

BULL, C R Swanscombe in Old Picture Postcards. 2005

BULL, C R Swanscombe (essay). 1986

DARBY H C & CAMPBELL, E M J The Domesday Geography of South East England. 1962

DUFF K L (ed) The Story of Swanscombe Man. 1985

EVERITT A The Community of Kent and the Great Rebellion 1640 - 1660. 1986

HASTED, E The History and Topographical Survey of the County of Kent. Vol II. second edition. 1797

MORGAN, P (ed) Domesday Book: Kent. 1983

PORTEUS, G H Dartford Country. 1985

RAIPH, E L Swanscombe through the Ages. 1964

ROOTES, A Front Line County: Kent at War 1939-1945. 1980

SPARVEL BAYLY J A A History of Swanscombe. 1875

SWANSCOMBE WOMEN Swanscombe Living Memories (2 vols). 1991, 1992

WALLENBERG, J K Kentish Place Names. 1931

Local History Folders under "Swanscombe" in Dartford Reference Library and under "KLSWA' in Gravesend Reference Library